Pursuing God

STUDY GUIDE + STREAMING VIDEO

ALSO BY MARGARET FEINBERG

The Organic God

The Sacred Echo: Hearing God's Voice in Every Area of Your Life

Scouting the Divine: My Search for God in Wine, Wool, and Wild Honey

Hungry for God: Discovering God's Voice in the Ordinary and Everyday

Wonderstruck: Awaken to the Nearness of God

Fight Back with Joy: Celebrate More. Regret Less. Stare Down Your Greatest Fears.

Live Loved

Live Fearless

Live Free

Pursuing God

ENCOUNTERING HIS LOVE AND BEAUTY IN THE BIBLE

STUDY GUIDE + STREAMING VIDEO
TWELVE SESSIONS

Margaret Feinberg

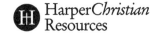

Harper*Christian*
Resources

Pursuing God Study Guide

Copyright © 2011, 2024 by Margaret Feinberg

This book is a compilation previously published as *Pursuing God's Love Participant's Guide* and *Pursuing God's Beauty Participant's Guide*. Copyright © 2011 by Margaret Feinberg.

Published in Grand Rapids, Michigan, by HarperChristian Resources. HarperChristian Resources is a registered trademark of HarperCollins Christian Publishing, Inc.

Requests for information should be addressed to customercare@harpercollins.com.

ISBN 978-0-17229-1 (softcover)
ISBN 978-0-17230-7 (ebook)

Special thanks to Evan Crass, Jennifer Rayner, and Maegan Stout and their small groups for their valuable feedback in the development of sessions one through six.

Cover design: Gearbox Design
Cover photography: Shutterstock
Interior design: Kait Lamphere

First Printing May 2024 / Printed in the United States of America

24 25 26 27 28 29 30 31 32 33 34 35 /TRM/ 16 15 14 13 12 11 10 9 8 7 6 5 4 3 2 1

Contents

A Message for Leaders

The twelve sessions of *Pursuing God* are designed to be accessible for people to grow in their knowledge of God and Scripture. Whether participants are still trying to figure out who God is or made the decision to follow Jesus decades ago, you'll find material that reaches them wherever they are in their spiritual journey.

Here are a few guidelines to help you and your group get the most out of this study.

MATERIALS NEEDED

Each participant should have his or her own study guide. Each study guide comes with individual streaming video access (instructions found on the inside front cover). Every member of your group has full access to watch videos from the convenience of their chosen devices at any time—for missed group meetings, for re-watching, for sharing teaching with others, or watching videos individually and then meeting if your group is short on meeting time and that makes the group experience doable and more realistic.

TAILOR THE STUDY TO YOUR GROUP

Groups are as diverse as the people in them. Some groups will want to watch one video session each week and complete the study in twelve weeks. Others may want to focus only on the six Genesis sessions and save the six Gospel of John sessions for another time (or vice versa). Some groups will want to watch the video and then discuss as a large group; others will prefer to watch the video together and then break into smaller groups to discuss. Tailor the study to what best suits your group.

SELECT AN EXPERIENTIAL ACTIVITY OR ICEBREAKER QUESTION IN ADVANCE

Each group session offers two options for getting started: an Experiential Activity or a selection of Icebreaker Questions. If your gathering is an hour or less, you may want to skip the activity or icebreaker question and dive right into the video so you have plenty of time for discussion. If your gathering is longer than an hour, select either the activity or one of the questions for your group.

Before the first meeting, read through all the experiential activities in the study. Select the ones you'd like to do and make a list of items you need to purchase, gather, or research.

Consider inviting a handful of participants to organize the experiential activity each week. This will encourage involvement and develop leadership skills of the participants.

SELECT DISCUSSION QUESTIONS IN ADVANCE

Each session includes a variety of discussion questions. Some questions focus on encouraging people to open up about their lives and others focus more on wrestling with Scripture and the material presented on the video.

More questions are provided than time will allow for most groups—don't feel like you have to ask every question. Before you gather, highlight the questions you want to focus on during the session. Select the questions best suited to the interests and objectives of your group. You may even want to develop a few questions of your own.

As you lead the discussion, remember that silence can be a friend. You may ask a question and be greeted with silence. Allow the silence to rest for a moment and see who speaks up. If you have a participant who is particularly quiet and you're asking an open-ended question that anyone could answer, consider calling on that person by name. Gently ask, "What do you think, Josh?" Try to avoid questions that lead to "yes" and "no" answers, and stay focused on learning more about God and deepening relationships.

Throughout the study, you'll discover quotes, scholarly observations, and various insights. Invite discussion on this content and see what develops.

ENCOURAGE PARTICIPANTS TO ENGAGE IN AFTERHOURS PERSONAL STUDIES (IF THEY CAN)

Each session includes five Afterhours personal studies. The goal of Afterhours is to challenge participants to keep diving deeper into the books of Genesis and John. Encourage participants to engage in the personal studies, but remember that not everyone will be able to do so.

Remind participants that even if they aren't able to do Afterhours, they're still welcome to be part of the study. If they can only do one personal study each week, encourage them to complete Day Five, which specifically prepares participants for the next group session.

STAY CONNECTED

Encourage participants to connect with Margaret on her website at www.margaretfeinberg.com, via Twitter @mafeinberg, or "like" her on Facebook. If you get a chance, take a photo of your group and submit it to be posted on the home page of her website. Email your photo to info@margaretfeinberg.com and include the name of your church or group.

PURSUING
GOD'S LOVE

Stories matter. Your story matters. My story matters. But the greatest story we will ever encounter is the story of God's love for us.

Stories were passed down orally long before they were written down. Genesis was written so the Israelites would know God and his presence and involvement in people's lives since the beginning of the world. Through the Genesis story, the Israelites are reminded how they became God's people and discover God's tremendous love for them.

Why pursue God's love?

From the foundation of the world, God created us for love. Pursuing God's love isn't just about receiving God's love but recognizing that we were made for the purpose of loving God and loving others. We are meant to experience God's love and become expressions of God's love in our world.

According to tradition, Moses wrote the first five books of the Bible (also called the Torah), including Genesis, though some scholars believe that Genesis is a collection of writings from different authors.

The first book of the Bible probably isn't the oldest written book in the Bible. Many scholars believe the book of Job predates Genesis. Yet the title of this book is derived from the very first word of Scripture, *beresheet*, which means "beginning." Does the word refer to the beginning of time, space, creation, or our planet? While the answer is debated, we know that Genesis is primarily the story of God and an expression of the divine desire for a relationship with humankind. Genesis is a story we need to hear because it teaches us about the depth and breadth of God's love for us.

My hope and prayer is that through these first six sessions you'll be reminded of the depths of God's love and faithful commitment to you.

Encountering God

Genesis 1–3

God loves us as we are, as he finds us, which is messy, muddy, and singing out of tune. Even when we've tried to be good, we have often only made matters worse, adding pride to our other failures. And the never-ending wonder at the heart of genuine Christian living is that God has come to meet us right there, in our confusion of pride and fear, of mess and muddle and downright rebellion and sin.[1]

—N. T. WRIGHT

Scripture is God's story. God is the central character, and God is the author of it all. Yet, as a loving God, we're invited into the divine story God has been writing since the beginning of time.

The opening chapters of Genesis are chock-full of stories that showcase the attributes of God. God is all-powerful, all-knowing, abounding in imagination, creativity, mystery, and wisdom. God is the source of life, strength, and goodness. God is immortal and transcendent. God has a plan and purpose. The first stories in Genesis remind us that even when we question, disobey, or doubt divine love, God continues pursuing us.

GETTING STARTED: Select One (10–15 minutes)

Experiential Activity: Imagining the Flavors of Eden

What you'll need:

- A variety of fresh fruits and vegetables
- Serving plates, forks, napkins

1. Visit a local supermarket that specializes in fresh produce. Buy a variety of fruits and vegetables. Be adventurous! Purchase some exotic fruits that you've never tried before.
2. Wash and prepare the fruits and vegetables prior to your gathering, or you may wish to leave everything whole and make cutting and peeling part of the group experience.
3. Discuss the following questions as you enjoy tasting your healthy snacks:
   - Which fruit is the most pleasing visually? Why?
   - Why do you think God created so many different types and flavors of fruits?
   - What emotions do you imagine God felt as creation unfolded?
   - After the man and woman were expelled from the garden, what are some of the things you think they missed most?

Icebreaker Question

*If you're not doing the experiential activity, choose **one** of the following questions to begin your discussion.*

- Imagine that you had the opportunity to stand alongside God on one of the days of creation. Which day of creation would you most like to experience and why?
- What kinds of activities help you appreciate the wonder of God's creation?
- What do you love about God the most?

VIDEO ONE: Encountering God (16 minutes)

As you watch the video, use the following outline to take notes on anything that stands out to you.

When I face times like those in life, the only thing I know to do is not give up.

In some ways, Genesis is the greatest love story ever told because it reminds us that God's love for humankind cannot be thwarted.

I apologized profusely, but hung up the phone with that sense of, "What have I done?"

As a holy and divine artist, God paints our world beautiful with the most loving attention to detail.

Whenever we focus on God's prohibitions rather than provisions, we can't help but doubt the goodness and generosity of God. We can't help but question God's love.

While the story in the garden is often referred to as "the fall of humankind," I can't help but think we need to rename it "God's rising."

GROUP DISCUSSION QUESTIONS (30–45 minutes)

1. What caught your attention or stood out most to you on the video?

Going Nowhere

2. The spiritual life is marked by seasons of growing and making great progress as well as those seasons when it doesn't feel like any progress is being made. Use the sentence starters to briefly describe both experiences.

   I know I'm growing spiritually when . . .

   I know I'm stalled spiritually when . . .

3. How do you typically respond when you mess up?

   Are you able to accept forgiveness (from God and others) and move on, or are you more likely to beat yourself up with regret and second-guessing?

   What helps you to move beyond your mistakes?

NOTABLE

Many scholars believe that Genesis was written for a people living in exile and meant to refute the false theological claims of the Babylonians. That it was written for a people who were discouraged and felt defeated. The first chapter of Genesis is a powerful declaration that God is the Lord of all.

The Story of God

4. When you read the Bible, do you tend to view what you're reading as a historical document, a scientific document, a theological document, a literary document, or some other way? Explain.

5. How does the way you tend to view the Bible affect the way you learn about God and grow spiritually?

6. Read Genesis 3:1–7. It's easy to recognize that Adam and the woman fell for the serpent's lie that God isn't good or doesn't really love them, but what relationships or situations tend to challenge *your* belief in God's goodness or love for you?

7. Deep down inside, do you really believe God loves you? Explain.

NOTABLE

Eve isn't named until Genesis 3:20, after encountering God.

God Rising

8. Overall, would you say you tend to focus more on God's prohibitions or God's provisions in your life? Mark your response on the continuum below. Briefly share the reason for your response.

I am always aware   I am always aware
of God's prohibitions.   of God's provisions.

9. Do you tend to focus more on your failings or on the redemptive healing and restoration God offers you? Mark your response on the continuum below. Briefly share the reason for your response.

I always focus more   I always focus more on
on my failings.   the redemptive healing and
                                                                                            restoration God offers me.

Why is it important to focus on God's rising more than our failings?

When have you most recently experienced God rising in your own life?

10. How are you actively and intentionally pursuing God's love in your life and your relationships right now?

At times, we need to shift our focus from our mistakes to God's rising—the ability of God to heal, redeem, and make a way for us. When we do, we find God's love pouring more readily to us and through us.

CLOSE IN PRAYER

Ask God to:

- Give you the spiritual eyes to see the wonders of creation.
- Provide a new appreciation for God's rising in your life.
- Open up new opportunities to both receive and extend God's love.

JUMPSTART

To prepare for the next group session, read Genesis 4 and tackle the Afterhours personal studies.

BONUS ACTIVITY

Take a quick photo! Before you close, take a picture of your group and email it to info@margaretfeinberg.com. Your group could be featured on the home page of www.margaretfeinberg.com.

Afterhours Personal Studies

Dive deeper into the book of Genesis by engaging in these five personal studies. If you only have time for one, choose Day Five, which will prepare you specifically for the next session.

DAY ONE: The Breathtaking Account of Creation

GENESIS 1:1–2:3

The opening chapter of Genesis provides a breathtaking account of the story of creation. This is the story of God bringing order to our world. The creation story is a powerful reminder that everything God creates has a purpose.

Each day of the creation story follows a pattern, which often includes *announcing, commanding, separating, reporting, naming, evaluating,* and *timing.* However, some days of creation provide exceptions to the pattern. For example, day two in the creation story is the only day in which God doesn't say, "It is good" (Genesis 1:6–8). Scholars differ on the explanation. Some suggest that day two isn't declared good because there is a separation between the heavens, or firmament, and the water below. They argue that any separation from heaven isn't good. Whatever the reason, it's worth paying attention to the exceptions found in the pattern used to describe creation.

1. Read Genesis 1. On day three, God says "It is good" twice. What do you think was good about creating the tree of life and the tree of knowledge of good and evil (Genesis 2:16–17)?

2. On which day of creation does God declare what he creates "very good" (Genesis 1:31)?

Why do you think this day receives a special declaration?

NOTABLE

On the first day, evening came before morning. Some believe this detail is reflective of the Jewish day, which begins at sundown rather than sunrise.

3. Which day of creation is mentioned three times, indicating its significance (Genesis 2:2–3)?

What is the first thing God creates that he sets apart as holy (Genesis 2:3)?

In what ways have you experienced the Sabbath as a holy day in your own life?

4. What is the only day of creation that does not include, "There was evening, there was morning" (Genesis 2:2–3)?

Why do you think this phrase is omitted?

 QUOTABLE

The Bible tells us how to go to Heaven, not how the heavens go."[3]

—Galileo Galilei

5. What obstacles in your life prevent you from entering God's rest?

In ancient culture, the sun, moon, and stars were often worshiped as gods. It is important to make a distinction between the objects that produce light and God as the source of light. Note the sequence of creation: God creates light itself on day one, but it isn't until day four that he hangs the sun, moon, and stars in the sky.

The creation story is laced with details that highlight the wonders of God. It teaches us that God exists within himself, triumphs over chaos, and is intimately involved with creation. While other gods threaten death and loss, our God is full of blessing. God's creation literally teams with life.

6. In which areas of your life do you need to experience God triumphing over chaos?

How do you hope to experience God's blessing in these areas?

Spend some time thanking God for any fresh insights or discoveries you made as you dove into the first chapter of Genesis. Ask God to give you the desire and time to dive deeper into the Scriptures over the upcoming week. Ask the Holy Spirit to illuminate Genesis as you read and study.

DAY TWO: Second Account of Creation

GENESIS 1-2

If the first chapter of Genesis provides a bird's eye view of the story of creation, then the second chapter provides a street-level view as it continues the story of creation, adding rich details to the creation of the garden and humankind.

An interesting shift in perspective takes place from Genesis 1 to Genesis 2. The first chapter of Genesis tells the creation story from God's perspective; the second chapter of Genesis tells the story from a human perspective. While Genesis 1:1 notes that in the beginning God created "the heavens and the earth," Genesis 2 reverses the order: "the earth and the heavens" (2:4).

1. Read Genesis 1–2. As you read, make a list of four to six differences you notice in the way the two chapters tell the creation story.

2. How does the Genesis 2 account of creation expand your understanding of God and the purpose of humankind? (*Hint:* See Genesis 2:15–17.)

NOTABLE

Men and women have the same number of ribs anatomically. But since Adam and Eve were the first people, it's always fair to wonder, did they have bellybuttons?

3. How should knowing that you're made in "the image of God" (see Genesis 1:26–27; 2:22–25) affect the way you interact and view the following:

Yourself

Others

God

4. Some scholars note a correlation between the words and phrases used in the story of creation and the words and phrases used in the Exodus story of the tabernacle. The tabernacle was a portable sanctuary, God's temporary dwelling place among his people before they were able to build a permanent temple. Scholars suggest that the temple is a smaller portrait of what God created in the beginning of Genesis. Look up the passages in the chart on the following page. What common words and phrases do they share?

PASSAGES	SHARED WORDS AND PHRASES
Genesis 1:31 and Exodus 39:43	
Genesis 2:1 and Exodus 39:32	
Genesis 2:2 and Exodus 40:33	
Genesis 2:3 and Exodus 39:43	

When God instructs the Israelites to build the tabernacle, God is renewing the vision of the garden of Eden, the vision of God dwelling with humanity.

5. When are you most aware of God's desire to be with you? How do you respond when you sense the Spirit's tugging in your life?

God places Adam in the garden of Eden, which can be translated "pleasure" or "delight," and instructs him to enjoy the lush fruits and vegetables of the land, except for one: the fruit of the tree of knowledge of good and evil. Though the tree of life is mentioned first in the text, all the attention falls on the second tree—suggesting that mankind's desire for power is stronger than his hunger for life.

6. When do you feel most tempted by the desire for power?

Spend some time thanking God for the wonders and beauty of creation. Praise God for the care and love with which humankind was made. Ask God to increase your own desire for an intimate relationship with him as well as the abundant life he wants to give you.

DAY THREE: Facing Temptation

GENESIS 3:1-7

The third chapter of Genesis paints a beautiful portrait of God's love for us by demonstrating divine grace and provision for our lives. We meet God's adversary who takes the form of a serpent. The Genesis text never says that Satan is the actual snake in the garden, but in the Old Testament and the New, snakes are sometimes used to describe evil people or nations. However, in the last book of the Bible, Satan is described as a snake (Revelation 12:9, 13–15). Satan could have chosen to take the form of any animal, but chooses a wise, crafty reptile.

1. Read Genesis 3:1–3 and compare it to Genesis 2:16–17. How does the serpent distort God's instructions?

NOTABLE

The Hebrew word for "knowing" is *yodea*, which can also be translated as a respectful reference to a divine being. The temptation of the serpent in Genesis 3:5 can be interpreted as a promise to become "divine beings, knowers of good and evil."

2. Read Genesis 3:4–5. The serpent is a smooth talker. In just a few sentences, he convinces the woman to doubt God's goodness and embrace disobedience. What do you think was most appealing to the woman about the serpent's argument in this passage?

Which aspect of the temptation would be the hardest for you to resist?

The serpent approaches the woman with a mixture of truth and falsehood. The woman turns to the tree, rather than God, to make her final decision. She finds the fruit is aesthetically pleasing and tasty. She shares the news with her husband. The Scripture doesn't detail their conversation, and so we are left to wonder: Did Adam protest? Did the woman disclose which fruit the tree was plucked from? Were the serpent's arguments enough to convince Adam? Did the woman add any arguments to persuade Adam to eat the fruit?

3. Read Genesis 3:6–7. In the space below, imagine and record the dialogue between the woman and Adam in which she convinces him to eat the fruit. For example:

THE WOMAN: "Honey, you'll never guess what I discovered in the garden today! The fruit on this one tree is sweeter and more delicious than anything we've eaten so far."
ADAM: "You know that I love fruit—which tree did you get it from?"

THE WOMAN:

ADAM:

THE WOMAN:

ADAM:

THE WOMAN:

ADAM:

Which argument do you imagine was most effective in convincing Adam to eat the fruit?

NOTABLE

Some scholars believe the tree of life extended life rather than granted immortality. Being removed from the garden prevented access to the tree. This intepretation explains why God never forbid Adam and Eve not to eat the fruit of the tree of life.

Though we don't know the details of the conversation between Adam and the woman, both ate the fruit. The consequences of their actions were just as God had warned—death entered the world. Their eyes were opened as they were given the knowledge of good and evil. In an instant, they experience something they've never encountered before: shame. What is shame? The painful feeling of embarrassment, humiliation, or distress resulting from the awareness of wrong, foolish, or ill-considered behavior.

4. What types of situations or encounters have caused you to feel shame?

5. The Bible is rich with promises about how God wants to remove our shame. Read Psalm 119:39; Romans 8:1–2; Romans 10:11; and John 8:1–11. How do these promises encourage you?

Spend some time asking God to reveal any interactions or incidents from the past for which you still feel shame. Ask God to remove any shame and saturate you with forgiveness, grace, and hope.

DAY FOUR: The Story of God

GENESIS 3:8-24

A crafty serpent convinces the woman of the ultimate lie, namely, that God is not good. She and Adam eat the fruit. Sin enters our world. Stripped of their innocence, the couple attempts to cover themselves. They reach for the bright green fig leaves—which are known to grow up to a foot in length—to create a covering. The couple is alienated from each other and God as they hide among the vegetation.

While the story of the garden is often called "the fall," a better name might be "God's rising." Remember that this is God's story: "In the beginning . . . God." While Genesis 3 highlights our sinful nature and a tragic decision on the part of humankind, the hero of the story is still God. A glimpse of God's plan for redemption emerges in the promise that one of the woman's offspring will crush the head of the serpent.

1. Despite their sin, God does not abandon Adam, the woman, or the garden. Read Genesis 3:8–13. What four questions does God ask?

GOD'S FOUR QUESTIONS	
1.	
2.	
3.	
4.	

If God already knows the answer to these questions, why do you think God chose to ask them anyway?

What does the interaction among God, Adam, and the woman reveal about God's love and his desire for a relationship with us?

2. Read Genesis 3:14–19. What does God curse in this passage? (*Hint:* See vv. 14, 17.)

3. Instead of cursing Adam or the woman, God makes several promises to them. List the promises God makes to the man and woman in the space below:

After God judges the serpent, the woman, and Adam, a subtle but significant shift takes place in the text. For the first time, the woman is given a personal name! She is called Eve, the mother of all the living. The name Eve is derived from the Hebrew word *chavah*, meaning "to breathe." This is the first sign of hope after the fall. God's redemptive work has begun. Eve will bear children. Many generations later one of her offspring will defeat evil forever.

A second sign of hope appears in God's provision for Adam and Eve. God takes on the role of fashion designer and creates clothing for them from animal skins. The scene foreshadows the central biblical truth that sin requires a sacrifice, which appears later in Scripture.

4. The third sign of hope is found in God's removal of Adam and Eve from the garden. Read Genesis 3:22–24. Why was driving the couple from the garden a sign of God's love and protection?

5. What are some unexpected ways in which you've experienced God's love and protection?

   How do you tend to respond to difficult situations in life before you recognize God's love and protection in those things?

6. How might the difficult things in your life right now actually be a sign of God's love and protection?

Adam and Eve are removed from the garden forever. The great loss is not the garden but God. Throughout the rest of the Old Testament, we never read about people wanting to return to the comforts of Eden; instead they long for God's presence. As Genesis continues to unfold, we keep seeing God rising—divine love and redemption appearing in the most unexpected circumstances and situations.

Spend some time reflecting on any areas of your life where you need to experience God rising. Ask God to increase your awareness of divine love.

DAY FIVE: Cain's Legacy

GENESIS 4

The story of Cain and Abel is a story of heartbreak—two brothers whose differences cause one to murder the other. In the wake of the fratricide, the story makes it clear that the descendants of Cain will continue to compound their sins until hope appears and God's people begin to love and obey him.

1. Read Genesis 4:1–16. Reflecting on Genesis 4:1–5, why do you think Cain's gift wasn't highly regarded by God?

2. Though Scripture does not specifically tell us, what do you imagine happened between Cain and Abel in the field on the day Cain murdered his brother?

Not only does the story of Cain teach us about the importance of love, forgiveness, and obedience, it also gives us an insight into temptations we face. God tells Cain, "If you do what is right, will you not be accepted? But if you do not do what is right, sin is crouching at your door; it desires to have you, but you must rule over it" (Genesis 4:7).

3. Read the passages listed in the chart on the next page. In the second column, note the wisdom each passage offers about handling anger. Then rate how difficult it is for you to apply this particular truth when you are angry. Use a scale of 1 to 10, with 10 being the most difficult.

SCRIPTURE	WISDOM ABOUT HOW TO HANDLE ANGER	LEVEL OF DIFFICULTY (1 TO 10)
Proverbs 15:1	*Ex.: Responding with gentleness can defuse anger.*	*Ex.: 7*
Proverbs 20:2		
Proverbs 21:14		
Proverbs 22:24		
Proverbs 29:11		
Ecclesiastes 7:9		
Matthew 5:21–24		
Ephesians 4:26–27		
James 1:20		

4. Reflecting on the Scriptures from the chart in question 3, list four to six ways Cain could have handled the situation differently.

Place a checkmark next to the passage that is most compelling for you. How might it help you to develop a healthier response to anger?

Whenever you encounter genealogies in Scripture, it's important to remember that they don't always include every single person who is born. They're more like a highlight reel. Biblical genealogies also serve more than one purpose. For example, they may trace lineage back to a common ancestor, establish continuity between biblical stories, demonstrate the legitimacy of a person for a particular office, or reveal God's redemptive work and favor in a person's life.

5. Read Genesis 4:17–26. What is the significance of the birth of Enosh?

What does it look like in your own life to call on the name of the Lord?

Spend some time in prayer asking God to reveal any areas of anger or unforgiveness in your life. Acknowledge what you've done or left undone. Ask God to forgive and heal you.

Call on the Name of the Lord

Genesis 4-11

God has made it a rule for Himself that He won't alter people's character by force. He can and will alter them—but only if the people will let Him. . . . He would rather have a world of free beings, with all its risks than a world of people who did right like machines because they couldn't do anything else. The more we succeed in imagining what a world of perfect automatic beings would be like, the more, I think, we shall see His wisdom.[5]

—C. S. LEWIS

In love, God gives us a choice. We are not forced to love God, but given a profound and life-shaping opportunity to love. At times we might be tempted to think that our lives would be easier or better if we were compelled to love God, but true love requires making a choice.

Will we love God? Or will we choose to love lesser gods? Will we choose to pursue God? Or will we choose to pursue someone or something else? God pursues us in love and we are given the opportunity to pursue God and divine love every day. When faced with this opportunity, the question becomes, what will we choose?

GETTING STARTED: Select One (10 – 15 minutes)

Experiential Activity: Discovering the Saint John's Bible

What you'll need:

- Information and images of the Saint John's Bible
- A laptop and video projector to display the images

1. Learn about the Saint John's Bible by visiting www.saintjohnsbible.org. Check the schedule to find out if the Saint John's Bible is on display in a city near you.
2. You'll find a brief video about the making of the Saint John's Bible by searching for "In the Beginning" and "St. John's Bible" on YouTube. Consider sharing the video with the group.
3. Talk about what you discover with the group.
4. Consider showing some of the images of the Saint John's Bible to participants and discuss the meaning of the symbols found in the illustrations. (Be sure to note if there are any restrictions on duplicating the image or if it is necessary to secure permission to reproduce the image.)
   - What inspires you about the Saint John's Bible project?
   - How do the illuminations help bring the Scriptures alive?
   - Which of the images shown is your favorite? Why?

Icebreaker Question

*If you're not doing the experiential activity, choose **one** of the following questions to begin your discussion.*

- Have you ever owned or encountered a Bible that was particularly meaningful to you? Describe what made it special to you.
- Anger can reveal itself in a variety of ways, including facial expressions, body posture, and tone of voice. When Cain becomes angry, his countenance falls. How can people tell if you're angry?
- What are some of the biggest challenges that technology is creating in your life? In your relationships?

VIDEO TWO: Call on the Name of the Lord (15 minutes)

As you watch the video, use the following outline to take notes on anything that stands out to you.

Donald Jackson wanted to create a Bible that captured the beauty and tradition of centuries of liturgy and carry it into the future.

While advancements in technology enhance our ability to absorb and share information and make our lives more convenient, they also create new challenges.

God doesn't ask questions to learn something new, but so we can learn something new about ourselves.

The man who refused to be his brother's keeper now has no one to keep him. The man who murdered now fears being murdered.

Technology is increasing and morality is decreasing.

We live in an age of great technological advancements, but maybe that's all the more reason to pursue God, to call on God.

GROUP DISCUSSION QUESTIONS (30–45 minutes)

1. Consider what you learned from God's love and pursuit of humanity through the Afterhours personal studies or on the video. What caught your attention or stood out most to you?

2. When have you been confronted with something inappropriate and unexpected because of technology?

   How did you respond to the situation?

God Pursues Abel

3. Read Genesis 4:1–8. What connection exists between the way Cain saw God and the way he treated Abel?

Why is it important to have a healthy, accurate view of God?

4. When has a distorted view of God affected the way you see and treat others?

NOTABLE

Abel's name in Hebrew is *Hevel*, meaning "vapor" or "breath," which may be a foreshadowing of his short lifespan.

5. Read Genesis 4:9–16. What encouragement do you find in God's protection of Cain in the midst of his punishment (vv. 13–15)?

What does God's protection reveal about divine love and grace?

QUOTABLE

"Here through our story, the Bible is expressing one of the most profound, if saddest, truths in the history of religions when it shows how an originally well-intentioned act of divine worship could become the cause of the first murder committed by man."[6]

—Nahum M. Sarna

An Ancient Genealogy with Modern Implications

6. Participants can take turns reading the following passages aloud: Genesis 4:17–26; Matthew 18:21–22; Luke 17:3–4. Reflecting on the song of vengeance by Lamech (Genesis 4:23–24) and the Gospel passages, how do you think Jesus would respond to Lamech's song?

7. What types of situations are most difficult for you to choose to forgive?

Why is forgiveness important to you?

Calling on the Name of the Lord

8. What does it specifically look like for you to call on the name of the Lord while engaged in the following activities? (For example: *I prayerfully consider how much time to spend on social media.*)

Using social media such as Facebook or Twitter

Using your mobile phone

Shopping online

Surfing the internet

Other

9. Apart from the use of technology, how do you call on the name of the Lord in daily life?

10. What prevents you from calling on the name of the Lord more often?

The story of Cain and Abel as well as the genealogy tucked into Genesis 4 are powerful reminders that though sin abounds, we can choose to be people who call on the name of the Lord. We do not have to allow sin to get the best of us—we can call on God and be the people who pursue God's love.

CLOSE IN PRAYER

Ask God to:

- Bring to mind any areas of unforgiveness for which you need to be forgiven.
- Give you wisdom and grace as you use technology.
- Prompt you to call on the name of the Lord more often.

JUMPSTART

To prepare for the next group session, read Genesis 12–23 and tackle the Afterhours personal studies.

Afterhours Personal Studies

Dive deeper into the book of Genesis by engaging in these five personal studies. If you only have time for one, choose Day Five, which will prepare you specifically for the next session.

DAY ONE: Walking with God among the Generations

GENESIS 5

Genealogies in the Bible often follow a pattern. When this happens in a genealogy, it's important to pay attention to any deviations from the pattern.

1. Read Genesis 5 and note how the narrative uses the basic genealogy pattern: naming a man who lives so many years, has children, and then dies. Use the chart to document the deviations from this basic genealogy pattern and why you think each deviation might be significant.

SCRIPTURE	DEVIATION	SIGNIFICANCE
Genesis 5:3		
Genesis 5:24		
Genesis 5:29		
Others?		

2. What are some specific times in your life when you've experienced that kind of close and intimate relationship with God that Enoch experienced?

3. What does it look like to walk with God in your own life?

NOTABLE

Enoch's name means "dedicated, vowed, or trained." Enoch is listed seventh, a position often given special attention in biblical genealogies.

4. What recent opportunities has God given you to be a source of comfort—like Noah (Genesis 5:29)—for others?

Enoch walks with God and doesn't die in the same way the others do. Enoch gives us the hope that if we walk with God, we too can get a reprieve from death. And Noah, a man whose name means "comfort," gives us the hope that we too can have a reprieve from living under a curse. This genealogy suggests that though we live in a fallen world and all of us will eventually die, we can find a reprieve if we walk with God just as Enoch and Noah did.

Spend some time in prayer asking the Lord to increase your desire for a more intimate and close relationship with God. Ask for opportunities to be a source of comfort to others. Keep your eyes open for the ways God answers that prayer over the upcoming week.

DAY TWO: The Call to Build an Ark

GENESIS 6

At the end of the Genesis 5 genealogy, we meet a new character, Noah, and enter into a new chapter in the story of God's redeeming work in the world. Sin still abounds on the earth, but God raises up a new generation who will call on the name of the Lord and walk in righteousness.

Before Noah's story begins, there is a brief "aside" in Genesis 6:1–4 about the Nephilim. Theories abound about this mysterious group, whose only other mention in Scripture is found in Numbers 13:32–33. The Hebrew word *nephilim* can be translated "fallen ones." Some believe they were supernatural beings from God's heavenly court, which would make the Nephilim fallen angels. Others believe they are descendants of Seth who are marked by their rebellion. In any case, their association in the Bible is not a positive one.

1. Read Genesis 6:1–22. What parallels do you see between this description of the corruption of humanity (Genesis 6:1–8) and that which appeared in Genesis 4:16–26 (also discussed in the video)?

2. Noah is described as a righteous man. How do Noah and his family compare with the corrupt people around them? (*Hint:* See Genesis 6:5, 8–9, 11–12.)

When have you found yourself standing in stark contrast to those around you because of your righteous choices?

How did you handle the situation?

NOTABLE

In Genesis 6:9, "blameless" can be translated as being "whole" or "complete."

3. Noah was surrounded by unrighteous people but chose to live righteously. When it comes to the unrighteous people in your life right now, would you say you are the influencer or the one being influenced?

4. Reflecting on Noah's story, in which relationships of your life do you need to invest more time and energy in order to be a godly influence? What personal relationships do you need to reevaluate because you're being negatively influenced by them?

Throughout the Noah narrative, God is not angered as much as grieved. Creation opposes divine purposes. Evil reigns in people's hearts. The pain experienced by Eve as described in Genesis 3:16 is now felt by God. *'Atsab*, the Hebrew word used for Eve's "pain" in Genesis 3:16, is the same word translated as "grieve" (NASB) to describe God's anguish in Genesis 6:6. God is not an angry tyrant but a loving Creator who grieves over what has become of creation.

5. In the first session, we learned that God has power over chaos. In the story of Noah, God uses a recognized force of chaos—raging waters—to overcome the human chaos of violence. What does God's care for Noah, his family, and all the living creatures reveal about God's love for creation and humanity?

In Genesis 6:18, the word "covenant" (*berit*) appears for the first time. God doesn't just establish *a* covenant; he calls it "my covenant." God takes ownership of the covenant. God promises to preserve Noah but, as part of the covenant, Noah must follow God's specific instructions and build an ark. The building of the ark is not only outrageously expensive but takes years to complete. This is an epic moment—not just for Noah and his family but for all of us. If Noah chooses to disobey, sleep in, or wait for plan B, God's divine purpose to bring salvation through the future generations will be derailed. Fortunately, Noah chooses to obey.

Consider the people you spend the most time with each day. Ask God for the strength and grace to be a reflection of God's righteousness in their lives. Look for opportunities to serve, practice generosity, and demonstrate God's love in tangible ways.

DAY THREE: All Aboard the Ark

GENESIS 7–9

Building the ark was a monumental challenge, but imagine stepping aboard the ark with hundreds (if not thousands) of noisy, stinky animals. The gathering of the animals for the ark raises all of kinds of questions. Instead of addressing these concerns, the story focuses on God's intimate involvement and Noah's faithful obedience.

1. Read Genesis 7–8. (You may want to skim 6:14–22 first.) Reflect for a moment on the enormity of this project as well as some of the concerns, conflicts, and humorous situations that would emerge along the way. What questions does the story of the ark, the animals, and Noah's family raise? (For example: *What did Noah do when one animal tried to eat another?*)

2. Noah obeys God in the monumental project of building and filling the ark. What does this reveal about how he probably responded to God in smaller, day-to-day things?

Is it easier for you to trust God with a monumental project or smaller, day-to-day activities? Why?

QUOTABLE

"The Bible contains much that is relevant today, like Noah taking 40 days to find a place to park."[7]

—Curtis McDougall

After Noah, his family, and all the animals board the ark, God closes the door behind them. Imagine Noah's wife turning to confirm the door closed on its own after hearing it slam, and feeling goose bumps run and up down her spine. After months of preparation, building, and waiting, the moment arrives and God is still with them. The door-closing demonstrates the divine presence and protection as they embark into the unknown.

Genesis 8 begins with the words, "God remembered Noah." This remembering isn't just a fleeting thought that eight people are seasick inside a wooden contraption being tossed to and fro in the greatest flood the world has ever seen. The Hebrew word for remember, *zkr*, signifies God acting on a commitment because of a covenant relationship. God alone controls the flood and has not forgotten the promise to Noah.

As the waters subside, Noah releases two birds from the ark to find out whether or not it's safe to leave the vessel. The first is a raven, a bird eventually considered unclean according to the law of Moses (Deuteronomy 14:14). The second is a dove, a bird eventually considered clean according to the law of Moses and acceptable for the poor to offer as a sacrifice (Leviticus 5:7). When the dove is released and fails to return, Noah knows the land is dry. Noah's first act on dry land is to build an altar and worship. God promises to never again destroy every living thing with floodwaters and marks the covenant with a rainbow.

While the word "rainbow" is used to describe the sign of God's covenant in Genesis 9:13, the actual word in Hebrew is "bow," signifying a hunting instrument or battle weapon. This highlights a bit of irony since one of the reasons God destroyed humanity was because of their violence (Genesis 6:13). God turned a sign of hostility into a symbol of reconciliation and peace by symbolically hanging a divine bow in the sky.

3. Read Genesis 9:1–18. Then look up the Scriptures passages in the following chart and note the parallels between Adam and Noah.

SCRIPTURES	PARALLELS BETWEEN ADAM AND NOAH
Genesis 3:8 and Genesis 6:9	
Genesis 2:19 and Genesis 7:15	
Genesis 1:28–30 and Genesis 9:1–7	
Genesis 3:17–19 and Genesis 9:20	
Genesis 3:6 and Genesis 9:21	
Genesis 3:7 and Genesis 9:21	

What do the parallels reveal about God's faithfulness and love of humanity?

Though we aren't given the exact timing, Genesis 9:18 marks a shift in the story of Noah. Through Noah's sons—Shem, Ham, and Japheth—the earth is repopulated. Noah follows in the footsteps of Adam and cultivates the land. He becomes a vintner, growing grapes. After processing the harvest, Noah over-imbibes and becomes drunk. The Scripture says he then uncovers himself in his tent.

Just a few chapters earlier, Adam and Eve were running through the garden without clothes. After the fall, people are increasingly aware of their nakedness. Ham sees his father and tells his brothers, Shem and Japheth, who take a garment, walk backward, and cover their father without seeing him naked. Scholars debate why Ham's actions are considered so despicable. Some argue that Ham saw Noah and his wife being intimate and told the details to his brothers. Others suggest that something sexual happened between Ham and his father. Others suggest that something sexual happened between Ham and his mother.

The text is blank on this detail. All we know is that Ham did not preserve the dignity of his father as his brothers did. When Noah awakes, he curses Canaan, Ham's son. In other words, Ham's entire family line is affected. A man God used to bring comfort and to lift the curse of working the soil ends up cursing his own family line.

4. Read Genesis 9:19–29. What surprises you most about the ending of Noah's life story?

5. What warnings from the end of Noah's life story are most applicable in your own spiritual walk right now?

6. What aspects of Noah's character—obedience, hard work, faith, courage, hope, resilience, and patience—do you feel most in need of? Why?

QUOTABLE

"Noah was a brave man to sail in a wooden boat with two termites."

—Unknown

Spend some time reflecting on Noah's story. Ask God to develop the character traits that you most appreciate about Noah in your own life.

DAY FOUR: Constructing a Tower to Heaven

GENESIS 10–11

Genesis 10 records a genealogy of the sons of Noah. This genealogy reminds us that even in the darkest of times, God still has a redemptive plan. Though the world dies in the flood, God mercifully saves one family. Through their line, humanity is recreated.

1. Read Genesis 10. Reflecting on what you've learned so far about genealogies from the video as well as the personal studies, what catches your attention in this genealogy?

While the initial listing of Shem, Ham, and Japheth (10:1) is consistent with their first mention in Genesis 5:32, the genealogy takes a turn by unpacking Japheth's family line first (10:2–5), then moving on to Ham (10:6–20) and Shem (10:21–31).

Japheth's family line is the least developed genealogy and thus the most challenging to interpret. Some scholars believe Japheth's descendants were allies of Israel. Genesis 9:27 describes Japheth sharing the tents of Shem, hinting that they shared the land. Meanwhile, other scholars believe Japheth's line traces to the Philistines, who eventually competed against the Israelites for land and power.

Ham's family line centers on Canaan and the political and theological effects of the curse. While Shem and Japheth are blessed, Canaan is cursed, pointing toward the power struggle between Israel and Canaan that will unfold for years to come.

Shem's line leads intentionally and directly to Abraham. Ten generations are listed between Shem and Abraham, the same number of generations listed between Adam and Noah in Genesis 5. These genealogies take on new significance in Luke 3:34–38 when the lineage of Jesus is traced back to Shem, Noah, and Adam.

The genealogy details many territories, clans, nations, and languages, hinting that the people are becoming diverse in their geography, ethnicity, communication, and culture.

One of the most interesting characters in the genealogy is Nimrod, the grandson of Ham, whose name means "we shall rebel." Genesis 10:8 tells us that his name fit his aggressive reputation. He was known as a tyrant. Rather than build altars to God, he built cities. His empire included all of Mesopotamia. Nimrod is noted for founding the godless cities of Babylon and Nineveh. Years later, these cities bring Israel to her knees, yet even here we are reminded that nothing is beyond the reach of God's redemptive plan.

As people multiply, they move—some head to the coast, others settle inland. Overall, the genealogy highlights God's ongoing blessing to be fruitful, multiply, and fill the earth (Genesis 9:1).

2. Read Genesis 11. As the people journey east, they settle on a plain in Shinar (11:2). This is not the first time people are described as moving eastward. What role does "east" play in each of the following passages?

   Genesis 3:24

   Genesis 4:16

   What kinds of situations tempt you to head "east" rather than toward a closer, more intimate relationship with God?

After the flood, people settle in southern Mesopotamia where the building materials are different than those in Israel or Egypt. Any stones in the area had to be carried in at great expense and labor. Thus, the people turn to bricks for their most valuable buildings.

The region was also known for its ziggurats, massive monuments that resemble pyramids, which were dedicated to various deities. The main architectural features of a ziggurat are a stairway or ramp that leads to the top of the building and a small area at the top of the structure—a guest room—to accommodate the god. A ziggurat was built to make it easier for a deity to descend, accept worship, and bless the people. This may have been what the people had in mind when they dreamed up their construction project.

NOTABLE

In Genesis 11, there's a play on words in the Hebrew expression, "Let us make bricks" (*nilb na*) in verse 3 and "Let us confuse" (*nab la*) in verse 7, implying that though the people had one plan, God had another.

3. Why do you think God took offense at people building a tower?

What are some examples of offensive towers people still build today (in other words, specific ways we try to manipulate or replace God)?

4. How many times does the phrase "let us" appear in Genesis 11:4?

What does this phrase reveal about the people's focus?

What happens in your own life when you shift your focus away from God?

The people want to penetrate divinity in order to lay hold of divinity themselves. The people build a tower with the expectation that God will come down, and when he does, it's not with the response they had hoped. God recognizes that people have crossed a threshold of corruption and sin which cannot be undone. Humanity refuses to live within its God-given boundaries.

NOTABLE
The confusion unleashed at the tower of Babel is reversed at Pentecost. Read Acts 2:5–18 to find out how the Spirit empowers people to unite and understand one another.

5. In what ways are the people struggling to live within their God-given boundaries?

In what ways do *you* struggle to live within God-given boundaries?

Rather than ban the building of future towers or send a plague on the builders, God cuts to the heart of the issue: he confuses the people's language. The result is that cooperation is impossible and scattering becomes inevitable. The place is named Babel, meaning "confusion," which sounds like the Hebrew word for Babylon.

The story of the tower of Babel carries poetic beauty and irony. The story begins with all the earth speaking one language and ends with everyone speaking different languages. The people who want to make a name for themselves end up with the name "confusion."

Throughout the book of Genesis, sin and corruption find new outlets and expressions:

- Adam and Eve choose to eat the forbidden fruit in an effort to be like God.
- Cain falls into temptation and murders his brother because God did not regard his offering.
- Before the flood, people are overcome by evil in their minds and actions.
- After the flood, humankind tries to build its own path to God's presence.

Before Genesis 11 comes to a close, we are offered a final genealogy of Shem, one of Noah's sons. This is the genealogy that links Noah to Abraham and sets the scene for Abraham's unique calling by God: he will father a nation that will bless the nations.

6. Reflecting on the first eleven chapters of Genesis, what have you learned about the nature of God and God's loving care for humanity and creation?

Spend some time prayerfully considering any offensive towers that you may have built in your own life. Ask the Holy Spirit to illuminate any areas where you may be depending on yourself rather than God. Ask for forgiveness and the grace and strength to tear down those towers and humbly depend on God.

DAY FIVE: The Challenges of Choosing to Believe

GENESIS 12

Abraham's journey is filled with highs and lows with a few loop-de-loops thrown in. God uses an infertile couple to fill the earth with people who are called to know and love the Creator. Nearly everything that happens in the life of Abraham traces back to the first three verses of Genesis 12. The highlights and lowlights of his journey either demonstrate a movement toward the fulfillment of these promises and blessings or an obstacle diverting Abraham away from them.

1. Read Genesis 12:1–3. God's call on Abraham in this passage contains seven elements, which is the symbolic number for totality or completeness. Use the chart to identify the seven elements of God's covenant with Abraham.

THE SEVEN ELEMENTS OF GOD'S COVENANT WITH ABRAHAM	
1.	
2.	
3.	
4.	
5.	
6.	
7.	

Abraham probably never expected the Promised Land to be full of famine. Rather than call out to God about how to handle the situation, Abraham decides to travel to Egypt. While most areas depend on rainfall for their water, Egypt depends on the annual flooding of the Nile, making it less susceptible to famine than other areas. It's worth noting that Abraham doesn't build a single altar along the way, an indication that seeking God doesn't mark his journey.

2. Read Genesis 12:4–20. God promises Abraham land, but instead of laying hold of the land, Abraham is confronted with famine. When have you experienced God leading you into a situation that was different than you expected?

How did your response compare to Abraham's?

After arriving in Egypt, Abraham deceives the authorities. Abraham and Sarah barely escape with their lives. The story of Abraham in Egypt foreshadows the story of God's people in Egypt centuries later.

3. The Scripture passages in the following chart compare the story of Abraham to other stories in the Old Testament. Use the space provided to note the parallels between these stories and Abraham's story.

SCRIPTURES	PARALLELS
Genesis 12:10 and Genesis 47:4	
Genesis 12:12–15 and Exodus 1:11–14	
Genesis 12:17 and Exodus 7:14–12:30	
Genesis 12:16 and Exodus 12:33–36	

How does paying attention to parallels between stories enhance your appreciation of Scripture and deepen your understanding of God's Word?

4. After all God had done to protect and provide for Abraham—defeating kings, rescuing Lot, instituting the covenant of circumcision—Abraham still thinks he needs to take matters into his own hands. What mental arguments do you imagine Abraham used to justify the deception?

Have you ever taken matters into your own hands and chosen deception rather than honesty? What was the result?

Spend some time prayerfully considering if there are any areas of dishonesty in your life which you need to confess. Ask God for wisdom on how to best handle the situation.

The Pursuit, the Promise, and the Provision

Genesis 12–23

Although I don't know the tantalizing details that surrounded Abraham's launch into the adventure of knowing God, it's clear that something stirred in his heart. The small candle of his conscience must have been lit, his spirit must have sought to draw near to the one true living God, because God leaned out of heaven and invaded Abraham's life.[8]

—ANNE GRAHAM LOTZ

Faith isn't easy. Faith asks us to respond to divine direction rather than just the observable data. Faith invites us to embrace the goodness of God even when what we see around us suggests God doesn't have our best interests at heart. Faith asks us to resist taking matters into our own hands. Faith challenges us to believe the impossible. And faith asks us to live courageously, abandoning ourselves to God's care.

Abraham (early in his story known as Abram) chooses to embark on an unforgettable journey of faith. Through Abraham's story, we discover much about God. We learn how God pursues even the most unlikely people with unfathomable love. We discover that God remains true to his promises even when we fumble and stumble. And we watch as God provides—at times in the most unexpected and outrageous ways. Abraham's story illuminates what it means to respond to the God who pursues us.

GETTING STARTED: Select One (10-15 minutes)

Experiential Activity: The Promise of God to Abraham

What you'll need:

- Hubble Telescope images of discoveries from space
- Photocopies of the images or a laptop and video projector to display the images

1. Visit websites such as www.hubblesite.org or check out books from the local library to find breathtaking images taken by the Hubble Telescope. (Be sure to note if there are any restrictions on duplicating the image or if it is necessary to secure permission to reproduce the image.) If you have access to a projector, the wallpaper gallery at www. hubblesite.org/gallery/wallpaper provides a spectacular collection.
2. Share these images with the group and then read Romans 1:20.
3. Discuss the following questions:
   - In what ways does nature display the invisible attributes of God?
   - How does God reveal himself through nature?
   - Imagine yourself as Abraham looking up at the sky and the stars above as God promised countless descendants (Genesis 15:5). What do you think Abraham felt as he listened to God's promise?
   - How do you think God continued to use quiet, star-filled nights to remind Abraham of divine faithfulness throughout Abraham's life?

Icebreaker Question

*If you're not doing the experiential activity, choose **one** of the following questions to begin your discussion.*

- When you meet someone for the first time, who is the person you're most commonly associated with? (For example: *You might be introduced as Mary's mom, Bob's boss, Karen's friend, Luke's brother, Pat's spouse.*) How does it make you feel to be so closely linked to this person?
- In what ways have you specifically sensed God pursuing you?
- Imagine God asking you, like Abraham, to leave everything that's familiar to travel to another part of the world. How would you feel about leaving everything and everyone you know and love?

VIDEO THREE: The Pursuit, the Promise, and the Provision (12 minutes)

As you watch the video, use the following outline to take notes on anything that stands out to you.

Not only does Abraham* not know God, but he isn't exactly a prime candidate to be chosen.

Abraham's life story is testament that God is true. Despite mistakes and setbacks, God fulfills all the promises.

God doesn't take away anything from Abraham that isn't replaced.

To serve the God of Abraham means that we also serve a God who pursues, promises, and provides.

Abraham's story reminds us that no matter where we are, even if we're living in the land of Ur, a place representative of serving false gods, a place marked by loss, pain, and poor choices, God pursues us there.

---

* For ease of use, Margaret uses the names Abraham and Sarah, though they are first known as Abram and Sarai.

GROUP DISCUSSION QUESTIONS (30 – 45 minutes)

1. Consider what you learned about the pursuit, promises, and provision of God from the Afterhours personal studies or on the video. What caught your attention or stood out most to you?

QUOTABLE

"Ur belonged to the moon god (incidentally, called Sin). The Sumerians could boast of running water and the beginning of a written alphabet. Abram and his people could have enjoyed a pleasant and rather uneventful life there in the Fertile Crescent."[9]

—Celia Brewer Sinclair, author and lecturer

The Pursuit of God

2. God chooses Abraham—a man who doesn't know God from a coconut—to be the father of our faith. What encouragement do you find in God's selection of Abraham?

3. Do you tend to think of your own spiritual life in terms of God pursuing you or of you pursuing God? Why?

4. In what specific ways have you experienced God pursuing you recently?

NOTABLE

The word "bless" appears only five times in the first eleven chapters of Genesis, then occurs five times in the first three verses of Genesis 12, which describes Abraham's calling.

The Promises of God

5. Read Genesis 12:1–3. How do you think you would respond if God asked of you the same thing he asked of Abraham?

6. Which of God's promises to Abraham is one you would like to claim as your own right now? Why?

7. The calling of Abraham and the promise God gives him hinge on a ruthless abandonment of what is familiar and comfortable. In what ways has God called you to abandon what is familiar and comfortable?

8. The story of Abraham raises important questions about faith:

In what or in whom do you place your faith?

What do you have faith for?

What shakes your faith?

What strengthens your faith?

QUOTABLE

"Why and how does one continue to trust solely in the promise when the evidence against the promise is all around? It is the scandal that is forced here. It is Abraham's embrace of this scandal that makes him the father of faith."[10]

—Walter Brueggemann

The Provision of God

9. When in the last six months have you experienced God providing for you or your family in a specific, meaningful way? In what way does God's provision demonstrate God's love for you?

10. In your own words, what does it mean to serve the God of Abraham?

The story of Abraham is a reminder that the journey of faith is paved with uncertainty. Yet that is the journey to which God calls us—one that is marked by the pursuit, the promises, and the provision of God.

CLOSE IN PRAYER

Ask God to:

- Provide a deeper understanding of the depths of love God has for you.
- Bring to mind any specific promises God had given you in the past.
- Strengthen your faith.

JUMPSTART

To prepare for the next session, read Genesis 24–27 and tackle the Afterhours personal studies.

Afterhours Personal Studies

Dive deeper into the book of Genesis by engaging in these five personal studies. If you only have time for one, choose Day Five, which will prepare you specifically for the next session.

DAY ONE: Tests and Trials of the Faith Journey

GENESIS 13–15

Though famine creates problems for Abraham while in Egypt, tensions now soar as a result of abundance. Abraham is not only rich, but *very* rich with all his livestock, silver, and gold. With so much wealth, conflict breaks out among the herdsmen who serve Abraham and Lot. There simply aren't enough natural resources to sustain all their animals in one place.

1. Read Genesis 13. For Abraham and Lot, the issues of abundance and scarcity lead to conflict. How has scarcity led to conflict in your life?

How has abundance led to conflict in your life?

2. Abraham seeks to be a peacemaker in the sticky situation with the herdsmen. What sacrifice does Abraham make to keep the peace (Genesis 13:8–9)?

Have you ever made a sacrifice in order to keep the peace in a relationship? Was it worth it? Why or why not?

Though Lot chooses the best land, God still promises to give Abraham the land. God instructs Abraham to walk the land as a symbol of his acquisition of the property. In response to God's renewed promises, Abraham builds an altar. In the wake of Abraham's generous peacemaking effort with Lot, conflict arises in the surrounding territories. War breaks out among the kings and Lot is taken hostage.

Throughout Genesis 14, the word "king" appears twenty-eight times. Though there are five kings of Canaan and four kings of Mesopotamia, as well as Melchizedek, king of Salem, we are reminded that there's only one true king—God, who rules over all.

3. Read Genesis 14. Abraham makes the decision to show loyalty to his disloyal nephew. Have you ever shown loyalty to someone who has been disloyal to you? What was the result?

QUOTABLE

"God orders Abraham to live his life before God in such a way that every single step is made with reference to God and every day experiences him close at hand."[11]

—Claus Westermann

4. The king of Salem, a place some scholars believe to be Jerusalem (Psalm 76:2), and the king of Sodom take different approaches when dealing with Abraham. How does the king of Salem greet Abraham (Genesis 14:18–20)?

   How does the king of Sodom greet Abraham (Genesis 14:21)?

   How are their greetings reflective of the land and people they lead?

5. When you think about the attitudes you display toward others, do you tend to have the attitude of the king of Salem or the king of Sodom? Why?

   What situations tend to bring out each attitude in you?

Abraham refuses the plunder offered to him by the king of Sodom. Though it's rightly his, Abraham knows that if he takes the booty, the presumptuous king will forever claim he made Abraham rich. God comes to Abraham in a vision and promises to be his protector and reward.

In Genesis 15, Abraham notes that despite all of God's promises and provision, he and Sarah are still childless. God assures Abraham that he will have a child from his own body. But that's not all!

After asking Abraham to admire the stars in the sky, God reminds him that God is the one who has brought him out of Ur and will give him the land. Abraham is skeptical. Why? Possibly because the promise isn't just about being given the land; it also means those who are in the land will have to be removed. Abraham asks God how he can know for sure the land will be his. God doesn't blink at the request. Instead, God enters into a covenant with Abraham in which God is the only responsible party.

God asks Abraham to bring a heifer, a goat, a ram, a turtledove, and a pigeon, and cut each animal in two. That evening the Lord appears as a smoking firepot and torch—images of purification—and passes between the pieces, establishing a covenant with Abraham.

NOTABLE

Genesis 15:17 describes a smoking cooking pot passing between the two halves of each animal. In the Bible, smoke, fire, and flames are often representative of God's presence. Consider Exodus 3:1–6; Exodus 19:16–18; and Revelation 1:12–16.

6. Read Genesis 15. Abraham's faith is renewed, but as the father of faith he is still living on the promises of God. What kinds of promises are you waiting for God to fulfill in your own life?

How has waiting shaped your:

Personal growth

Faith

Relationship with God

Spend some time reflecting on the promises God has made to you through the Scriptures. Thank God for the divine promises and the faithfulness displayed in your life.

DAY TWO: The Blessings and Judgments of God

GENESIS 16–18

Despite God's presence, provision, and the covenant promise of descendants, Abraham believes the only way he's going to get a son is to take matters into his own hands. Rather than listen to God's voice, he listens to the voice of his wife and agrees to sleep with her maid Hagar, whose name can be translated "forsaken." The result is Ishmael.

1. Read Genesis 16. In what ways did Hagar get shortchanged for her service to Sarah and Abraham?

   What does God's response to Hagar reveal about the nature of God (Genesis 16:9–11; 21:13–18)?

NOTABLE
Genesis 16:13 is the only known instance in Scripture where a human gives a name to God. It's an endearing moment as Hagar calls the Lord, "The God who sees me." The name is actually a play on words that can be interpreted as "the God who sees me" or "the God whom I see."

At the age of ninety-nine, Abraham—still called Abram—is visited by God again. God renews the promise and also gives Abram and Sarai their new names. Abram becomes Abraham, meaning "father of many." Sarai is the only woman in the Bible whose name is changed. She becomes Sarah, which can be translated as "princess."

2. Read Genesis 17. God makes a covenant with Abraham that can be divided into three parts—one for God, one for Abraham, and one for Sarah. Use the following chart to write down the main points of the covenant for each party.

RESPONSIBLE PARTY	INTRODUCTION	SCRIPTURE	COVENANT OBLIGATIONS
God	"As for me"	Genesis 17:4–8	
Abraham	"As for you"	Genesis 17:9–14	
Sarah	As for Sarah"	Genesis 17:15–16	

What one or two things make it difficult for you to walk blamelessly with God as Abraham did?

After establishing the covenant, God asks Abraham to be circumcised. Circumcision is a sign of being set apart. The male sex organ that enables God's people to have descendants is purified and set apart for God. The choice is permanent and irreversible.

While physical circumcision is crucial to God's covenant with Abraham, it is only a representation of a deeper issue—circumcision of the heart. God wants our hearts to be set apart for him. Scripture often makes reference to a circumcised heart or the idea that the Holy Spirit now writes the law of God on our hearts.

3. What do the following passages reveal about what it means to have our hearts circumcised to God?

> Ezekiel 44:7–9

> Jeremiah 31:31–34

> Romans 2:28–29

> Galatians 6:15

In what ways has your own heart been circumcised to God?

In Genesis 18, Abraham has two significant spiritual encounters in which he discovers the realities of the blessings and judgments of God. Abraham shows hospitality to three men who aren't your ordinary visitors. Then, Abraham has an encounter with God in which he pleads on behalf of Sodom.

4. Read Genesis 18. Why do you think Sarah laughed at the news of the angels?

Who else laughed at the promise of a child (Genesis 17:17)?

Have you ever laughed at something God promised you? If so, describe.

NOTABLE

The word for "outcry" found in Genesis 18:20–21 and 19:13 can be translated "outrage" and finds its roots in the anguished cry of the oppressed, the plea of a victim who has experienced injustice.

5. God approaches Abraham to discuss the fate of Sodom and Gomorrah. How do each of the following parties benefit from the discussion:

   God

   Abraham

   Lot and his family

   The people of Sodom and Gomorrah

6. In what ways does Genesis 18:1–15, 18–19 reveal the blessing of God?

In what ways does Genesis 18:20–33 reveal the judgments of God?

In what ways have you seen or experienced the blessings and judgments of God revealed in the last six months?

Spend some time reflecting on both the blessings and judgments of God in your own life. Thank God for both the blessing and judgments and the way they beckon you into a more intimate relationship with him.

DAY THREE: Lessons from Lot and Abraham

GENESIS 19-20

Following God's conversation with Abraham, two angels visit Sodom. When the angels enter the city, Lot is sitting at the city gate. In ancient cultures, the city gate was a symbol of authority and governing power. Lot's presence at the gate suggests he has some form of political authority in the city.

1. Read Genesis 19. How does Abraham's hospitality toward his visitors (Genesis 18:3–8) compare with the hospitality of Lot and Sodom (Genesis 19:1–10)?

Is the hospitality that you offer others more like Abraham's or Lot's?

NOTABLE

According to Mosaic law, two witnesses are needed to implement capital punishment. Two men are sent to Sodom to confirm the sinful behavior of the city.

2. While the sexual sin of Sodom is highlighted in Genesis 19, other passages of Scripture reveal additional sins committed by the inhabitants of the city. Use the chart to note what each passage reveals about Sodom's sins.

SCRIPTURE	SODOM'S SINS
Isaiah 1:10–17	
Jeremiah 23:14	
Ezekiel 16:49	

Reflecting on these passages and reputation of the city, which of the sins of Sodom do you tend to struggle with the most?

QUOTABLE

"[Lot] fancied he was dwelling in paradise, [but] was nearly plunged into the depths of hell."[12]

–John Calvin

Lot is now in a lose-lose situation. If he hands over his guests to the mob outside his door, they'll be raped and abused. Lot chooses to do the unthinkable; he offers his own daughters in their place. Some scholars believe that Lot's desire to save his guests—and not act as selfishly as the rest of Sodom—is what saves both him and his daughters.

A bit of irony is found in Lot's request to go to Zoar (Genesis 19:18–19). Zoar can be translated "small." Lot has been transformed from loving the big city to desiring a small town where he can get away.

3. What parallels do you find between the story of Lot and the story of Noah? Use the chart to note your observations.

SCRIPTURES	SIMILARITIES BETWEEN LOT AND NOAH
Genesis 6:13 and Genesis 19:13	
Genesis 6:8–9 and Genesis 19:12–13	
Genesis 7:6 and Genesis 19:24	
Genesis 7:16 and Genesis 19:10	
Genesis 9:22 and Genesis 19:32	
Genesis 6:5–8 and Genesis 19:29	

What surprises you about the similarities between these two men? Do you relate more to Lot or Noah? Why?

4. Read Genesis 20. The story of Abraham in Egypt (Genesis 12:10–20) parallels the story of Abraham in Gerar (Genesis 20:1–8). What are the differences and similarities between the two stories?

NOTABLE

Marriage to a half-sister was permitted in ancient times but later forbidden in the law of Moses, as described in Leviticus 18:9, 11 and 20:17.

5. One of the ironies captured in Genesis 20 is that Abimelek fears God more than Abraham does. In fact, here Abraham fears people more than he does God. In what areas of your life are you tempted to fear other people more than you fear God?

What temptations or failures do you find yourself wrestling with again and again?

Spend some time asking God to give you strength to resist any temptations that you face on an ongoing basis. Pray that God will send people around you who strengthen you, encourage you, and hold you accountable in a healthy and vibrant way.

DAY FOUR: Ultimate Faith

GENESIS 21–23

After years of waiting, the promised heir is born. Abraham names his son Isaac, as the angels instructed, and then circumcises him, as God instructed. The child whose name means "laughter" is now a source of laughter and joy for his parents.

The thrill of the moment does not last long as Sarah turns her eyes toward her maidservant, Hagar, and her son. Throughout Genesis 21, Ishmael's name is never mentioned; he is referred to only as "her son" and "the boy." This suggests Ishmael's secondary status to Isaac.

1. Read Genesis 21:1–21. The birth of Isaac opens up a blister of anger and resentment in Sarah toward Hagar and Ishmael. Hagar runs away. Stranded in the desert without water, she chooses to leave her child to die, but God intervenes—sending an angel and renewing the divine promise to her. Consider an area of your life or a difficult relationship that is so broken or hard it seems beyond help. How do you hope God might renew you or your relationship in a meaningful way?

In Galatians, Paul contrasts the faith of Hagar and Ishmael with the faith of Sarah and Isaac. Hagar and Ishmael are likened to the human effort to keep the laws of Judaism while Sarah and Isaac are likened to the promise and grace of God.

> **NOTABLE**
> The skin of water Abraham sent with Hagar into the desert would have held approximately three gallons.

2. Read Galatians 4:21–31. Use the following chart to note the areas of contrast between Hagar and Sarah.

SCRIPTURE	HAGAR	SARAH
Ex.: Galatians 4:23	Ex.: Bondwoman	Ex.: Freewoman

Reflecting on your own spiritual journey, do you tend to feel more like a child from the seed of Hagar or the seed of Sarah? Why?

Genesis 22 is one of the most challenging passages in the Bible. Everything God promises Abraham hinges on Isaac, yet God asks Abraham to sacrifice his own son. Abraham binds not only his son, but also the promises of God to the altar, and is willing to let them die. This scene reveals that Abraham had come to a place of being wholly surrendered to God.

3. Read Genesis 22. If God asked you to bind the most precious thing in your life to the altar, what would it be?

God does, in fact, ask us to surrender everything to him. What thoughts or emotions are you aware of when you consider the implications of surrendering the people or things that are most precious to you?

4. The story of Isaac and the story of Jesus share many of the same characteristics. Use the following chart to note the scriptural parallels between the two.

PASSAGES	PARALLELS BETWEEN ISAAC AND JESUS
Genesis 17:16 and Luke 1:31	
Genesis 17:19 and Matthew 1:21	
Genesis 18:10–15 and Matthew 1:1	
Genesis 18:12 and Luke 1:7	
Genesis 21:2 and Galatians 4:4	
Genesis 22:2 and John 1:14; 3:16	

PASSAGES	PARALLELS BETWEEN ISAAC AND JESUS
Genesis 22:2 and Matthew 26:39	
Genesis 22:6 and John 19:17	
Genesis 22:9 and Matthew 27:2	
Hebrews 11:17–19 and 1 Corinthians 15:4	
Genesis 22:4 and Matthew 12:40	
Genesis 25:5 and Hebrews 1:2	
Genesis 24:67 and Ephesians 5:25	

Which parallels between Isaac and Christ are most meaningful to you? Why?

The exchange between Abraham and Ephron in Genesis 23 over what to pay for a parcel of land is somewhat reminiscent of two people arguing about who will pick up the tab for dinner. Both men are wealthy and the sum of money is insignificant to Abraham, yet the tension persists.

NOTABLE

In Genesis 23:6, the Hittites call Abraham "mighty prince" or "prince of God." Though Abraham doesn't own any land in Canaan, they recognize God's blessing, provision, and protection on his life.

5. Read Genesis 23. The parcel Abraham purchases for Sarah's burial will be the only piece of the Promised Land he will own before his death. Though Ephron calls the 400 pieces of silver a small portion, his asking price is high; yet Abraham chooses to pay the full amount. Abraham refuses to receive the land as a gift, in part so that Ephron's heirs cannot reclaim it after Ephron dies. What does Abraham's concern for Sarah's burial—its location as well as its details—reveal about his care for her?

It's worth noting that the author of Genesis chooses to tell the story of Abraham immediately after the stories of the flood and tower of Babel. By arranging the stories in this way, the author reveals the fallen nature of humanity and then gives us great hope that God is still faithful and engaged in the world. God has a plan for humanity and the redemptive plan will continue to unfold. Even the sinfulness of God's people cannot thwart God's love.

Spend some time prayerfully considering anything in your life that God may want you to give up. Sometimes God asks us to give up something because it's sinful or a distraction in our lives. But sometimes it's for another reason. Isaac's story reveals that occasionally God asks us to give up something to ensure that we hold nothing else as precious as God, even if it's something good God gives us. Prayerfully reflect on any activities, relationships, commitments, or goals that you need to lay down in order to lay hold of God more fully.

DAY FIVE: A Bride for Isaac

GENESIS 24

God has been faithful to Abraham. Through a series of miraculous events, Isaac is born. In a place known as "The Lord Will Provide" or "Yahweh-jireh," Abraham is asked to sacrifice his own son. At the last moment, an angel intervenes and Isaac's life is spared. Yet for the promises of God to unfold in Abraham's life, Isaac must find a wife and have children of his own.

1. Read Genesis 24:1–14. Why do you think it was important to Abraham that his future daughter-in-law not be from among the Canaanites (Genesis 9:24–27) but from his homeland? (*Hint:* See Genesis 12:1–3.)

NOTABLE

Oaths in the ancient world varied greatly. The image of placing a hand under another person's thigh (24:2, 9) implies making an oath at the source of life (genitalia), which is poignant considering this oath involves Abraham's descendants.

Abraham's servant will be released from his commitment to bring back a bride if the woman herself is unwilling to follow him to Canaan. This exception suggests Abraham is moving forward by faith rather than presumption or force. Abraham recognizes the importance of the woman's choice and knows that if this is from God, then she will be willing to leave her homeland.

The servant's prayer for God's guidance in finding Isaac's future wife begins and ends with a request for God to show loving-kindness to Abraham. The Hebrew word for "kindness" is *hesed* and implies loyalty to a covenant relationship. It's also worth noting that this is the first prayer in the Bible asking for specific guidance. Isaac and Rebekah's meeting is bathed in prayer.

2. Read Genesis 24:15–28. God answers the prayer of Abraham's servant before he even finishes speaking it. Have you ever had God answer one of your prayers before you finished? If so, describe in the space below.

Overall, how would you describe your experience of God's timing in responding to your prayers? Place an X on the continuum to indicate your response.

God responds to   God responds to
my prayers quickly.   my prayers slowly.

Overall, how responsive do you feel God is to your prayers? Place an X on the continuum to indicate your response.

God is not very responsive   God is very responsive
to my prayers.   to my prayers.

How does your perception of God's timing and responsiveness to your prayers affect how you pray?

Rebekah's name can be translated "ensnaring beauty," and she's noted for her outer appearance as well as for being a virgin. She is an adolescent girl of marrying age and seems like an ideal selection for Isaac, but the real test will take place at the well (Genesis 24:15–16).

3. In what ways did Rebekah and her act of service at the well exceed the servant's request to God?

When was the last time God's answer to your prayers exceeded your expectations?

How did the experience affect your prayer life and relationship with God?

BONUS ACTIVITY

Calculate the following. If 10 camels each need 25 gallons of water and each gallon weighs 8 pounds, then how many pounds of water did Rebekah draw from the well? If an ancient jar for drawing water held 3 gallons, how many times did she have to lift a jar to provide water for all the camels?

Rebekah shares that she's the daughter of Bethuel, the son of Milcah. This is significant for the servant and Abraham. Bethuel is Isaac's cousin, so the divine providence of meeting Rebekah at the well far exceeds all the servant's expectations. Before the servant follows Rebekah back to her family's house, he takes a moment to pray and thank God.

The servant is a highly effective communicator who uses precise and persuasive language. The servant appeals to Laban's greed by describing Abraham's wealth and making it clear that Isaac is the only heir. Because Isaac will not marry among the Canaanites, Rebekah's heirs will be sole heirs. The servant shares the details of God's providence and appeals to the covenant with Abraham. In response, Laban acknowledges God's divine hand and agrees to allow Rebekah to make the journey with the servant and to marry Isaac.

4. Read Genesis 24:29–60. What is the servant's response to Laban (v. 52)?

How do you imagine your life might be different if it were marked by prayer?

The moment Isaac and Rebekah meet unfolds like a scene in a classic romantic movie. Rebekah is brave enough to leave everything except for a few maids and supplies to travel to an unknown land. Abraham made a similar journey years earlier.

5. Read Genesis 24:61–67. What do you imagine Rebekah felt as she left her family and homeland?

6. Rebekah takes a huge risk by leaving almost everything she owns to travel to a foreign land to marry an unknown man. Through her act of faith, she becomes part of a family line that will bless the entire world. What risk might God be asking you to take as an act of faith?

What do you imagine the blessing of taking the risk might be?

Isaac takes Rebekah into his mother's tent. As Isaac's wife, Rebekah is now the head woman of the household. Abraham is likely thrilled at the news of the arrival of his future daughter-in-law.

Spend some time reflecting on the risks God has been calling you to take in your own life. Ask God for the courage and strength to respond bravely and obediently.

When Love Goes Right and When Love Goes Wrong

Genesis 24-27

Christian Love, either towards God or towards man, is an affair of the will. If we are trying to do His will we are obeying the commandment, "Thou shalt love the Lord thy God." He will give us feelings of love if He pleases. We cannot create them for ourselves, and we must not demand them as a right. But the great thing to remember is that, though our feelings come and go, His love for us does not.[13]

— C. S. LEWIS

One of the many reasons I love Scripture is its captivating storytelling. Whether it's Eve facing off with a serpent in the garden or Noah staying afloat on the ark, the Bible is full of adventure. The pages are also laced with drama in stories such as Sarah vying with Hagar or the competition between Leah and Rachel. And there are stories of love: men and women who choose to love God wholeheartedly, as well as sparkling romances.

Two of the patriarchs, Abraham and Isaac, challenge us to consider what it means to love God and love others—not just for today or tomorrow but for a lifetime—and what it means to finish well.

GETTING STARTED: Select One (10–15 minutes)

Experiential Activity: Heart Collage

What you'll need:

- A large piece of poster board
- Superglue
- Red and/or white construction paper
- Colored markers
- Scissors

1. Provide each participant with a sheet of red and/or white paper, a pair of scissors, and a marker.
2. Invite everyone to cut out paper hearts. On each heart, write the name of something or someone you love. Be creative! Have fun!
3. Once all the hearts are created, invite participants to share what they wrote on their hearts and why.
4. Glue all of the hearts onto the poster board to make a collage.
5. Email a picture of your collage to info@margaretfeinberg.com and it may be posted on her site!

Icebreaker Question

*If you're not doing the experiential activity, choose **one** of the following questions to begin your discussion.*

- When you think about a great love story, which books or movies come to mind?
- What are some of the characteristics of a great love story?
- When you think about romantic love stories from the Bible, which ones do you think of?

VIDEO FOUR: When Love Goes Right and When Love Goes Wrong (18 minutes)

As you watch the video, use the following outline to take notes on anything that stands out to you.

Relationships aren't easy. Sometimes they get messy. Miscommunication occurs. Misunderstandings happen. Mistakes are made. Before we know it, a relationship we celebrated and treasured falls apart.

Abraham is a man whose life is marked by faith. He orients his life, his family, his everything on the promises of God. Meanwhile, Sarah is a woman whose body is transformed from barrenness into birthing a nation because of the power and promise of God.

Despite a wondrous beginning, a match made in heaven, Isaac and Rebekah's faith journeys and life together turn out much differently than one would expect. Rather than being a story of when love goes right, it quickly becomes a story of when love goes wrong.

Rebekah isn't given a memorial in Scripture, only a passing mention in Genesis 49 that she's buried alongside Isaac in the same place as Abraham and Sarah. To be a patriarch's wife and not be given a memorial in Genesis means you did not finish well.

Bottom line: Those who begin well do not always finish well.

My prayer for you is that God will give you the strength and courage to choose wisely today so that you may finish well, like Abraham, blessed and loved by God and those who know you best.

GROUP DISCUSSION QUESTIONS (30 – 45 minutes)

1. Consider what you learned about divine and romantic love from the Afterhours personal studies or on the video. What caught your attention or stood out most to you?

When Love Goes Right

2. Without naming anyone specific, describe a friendship in your life that exemplifies when "love goes right." What are some of the characteristics of that relationship? (examples: *honesty, consistent communication*)

3. Read Genesis 22:2–12. Based on this passage, what three to five words or phrases would you use to describe Abraham's love for God? (example: *sacrificial*)

4. To what degree would you say these same characteristics describe your love for God? A little, a lot, or somewhere in between? Place an X on the continuum to indicate your response. Then, if you feel comfortable, share the reasons for your response.

The characteristics of Abraham's love for God do not at all describe my love for God.

The characteristics of Abraham's love for God completely describe my love for God.

5. Read Genesis 23:1–9. What does this passage reveal about Abraham's love for Sarah?

6. Do you know anyone whose relationship shares characteristics with Abraham and Sarah's? If so, briefly describe. What is it you admire most about this couple? If you can't think of anyone, why do you think this kind of relationship might be so rare?

When Love Goes Wrong

7. Without naming anyone specific, describe a friendship in your life that exemplifies when "love goes wrong."

What issues caused the relationship to sour? (example: *lack of communication*)

8. Read Genesis 25:27–28; 27:1–13. What do you think contributed to the deterioration of Isaac and Rebekah's relationship?

What kind of tension does deception create in a relationship? A family?

What are the fruits of deception? (example: *mistrust*)

Finishing Well

9. On the video, Margaret says, "Those who begin well do not always finish well. And those who do not begin well do not have to end that way." Overall, would you say your current spiritual trajectory is leading you to become more like Abraham or Isaac? Place an X on the continuum to indicate your response. Then, if you feel comfortable, share the reasons for your response.

My spiritual trajectory is leading   My spiritual trajectory is leading
me to become more like Isaac.   me to become more like Abraham.

10. Margaret describes rebuilding her relationship with Carly. What thoughts or emotions are you aware of when you consider the possibility of taking steps to rebuild a broken relationship in your own life?

The love stories of Abraham and Sarah as well as Isaac and Rebekah remind us that in our lives we have some relationships in which love goes right and others in which love goes wrong. But as God's children we can make choices to make them right! This is true not only in our romantic relationships but also in our friendships and in our relationship with God.

CLOSE IN PRAYER

Ask God to:

- Illuminate any relationships that need restoration and healing.
- Bless and strengthen the relationships you've been given.
- Give you strength and tenacity to finish well in your own spiritual journey.

JUMPSTART

To prepare for the next session, read Genesis 28–36 and tackle the Afterhours personal studies.

Afterhours Personal Studies

Dive deeper into the book of Genesis by engaging in these five personal studies. If you only have time for one, choose Day Five, which will prepare you specifically for the next session.

DAY ONE: Reflecting on Abraham's Life

GENESIS 25:1–18

Abraham's life story comes to a close with the news that Abraham has taken another wife, Keturah, whose name means "incense" or "enveloped in fragrant smoke." Keturah's role is unclear because in Genesis 25:1 she is called a wife but in Genesis 25:6 she is referred to as a concubine. She may have become a full wife sometime during her life with Abraham. Abraham's kindness and generosity is displayed again before his death. Though he is not required to give anything to sons born to concubines, he chooses to show generosity anyway.

1. Read Genesis 25:1–11. Why do you think Abraham chooses to give his sons gifts when he is only required to give Isaac the full share of his inheritance?

What does Abraham's generosity reveal about his own character? His relationship with God?

In what ways do your actions display your inner character?

NOTABLE

Keturah bore Abraham six sons, the most notable of whom is Midian. Midian's descendants, the Midianites, make several appearances in the Scripture. Joseph is transported to Egypt by Midianite traders (Genesis 37:28) and Moses marries into a family headed by the priest of Midian named Jethro (Exodus 3:1; Numbers 10:29). The Midianites partake in the disaster at Baal Peor along with the Moabites, and Moses orders their extermination in Numbers 31.

2. How is Abraham described before his death in Genesis 25:7–8?

How is this description a fulfillment of God's promise? (*Hint:* See Genesis 15:15.)

How would you like to be described when you're at the same stage of life as Abraham?

3. Abraham's story is reflected on throughout both the Old Testament and the New Testament. Look up the following passages, then use the chart to note what each one reveals about Abraham. Place a checkmark next to any of the statements that might be true of you right now.

SCRIPTURE	INSIGHT ABOUT ABRAHAM	✓
2 Chronicles 20:7		
Isaiah 29:22		
Matthew 1:1–16		
John 8:56		

What insights did you discover in considering how your life is similar to or different from the descriptions of Abraham's life?

4. Reflecting on what you've learned so far, sum up the life of Abraham in ten words or less.

5. Read Genesis 25:12–18. Isaac and Ishmael bury Abraham next to Sarah. How is the description of Ishmael's descendants a fulfillment of the prophecies and promises regarding Ishmael (Genesis 16:12; 21:18)?

6. What is the most important lesson you've learned about Abraham's life that applies to your own situation right now?

Spend some time asking God for greater faith—like that demonstrated by Abraham—to follow God into the unknown.

DAY TWO: Sibling Rivalry

GENESIS 25:19-28

For God to fulfill the promise to Abraham—to make him the father of many nations through his son, Isaac—Rebekah needs to have a child. But, like Sarah, Rebekah is barren.

1. Read Genesis 25:19–28. How does Isaac's response to his wife's barrenness differ from Abraham's response to Sarah's barrenness (Genesis 16:1–4)?

NOTABLE

The prophecy concerning Jacob and Esau in Genesis 25:23 is not only fulfilled throughout the history of Israel but even during the birth of Christ. Herod was a descendant of Esau.

2. How long does Isaac have to wait for God to answer his prayer for a son? (*Hint:* See Genesis 25:20, 26.)

What does such a long period of waiting reveal about Isaac's faith?

What, for you, is the hardest part of waiting for God to answer a prayer?

3. Several months after Rebekah conceives, she is unsettled when she experiences a jostling in her abdomen. In essence, Rebekah asks God, "Why is this happening to me?" Have you ever asked God a question like this in the midst of a struggle? What was the response?

NOTABLE

Like many people in the Bible, Isaac's sons' names have meanings that reflect their appearance or life story. Esau can be translated as "red" or "hairy" and Jacob means "heel" or "supplanter."

Jacob is described as being a "peaceful man" who lives among the tents (Genesis 25:27 NASB). The Hebrew word here is *tam* and can be translated "civilized." In other words, while Esau enjoys the outdoors, Jacob prefers a more cultured, refined lifestyle.

4. What signs of rivalry emerge between Jacob and Esau in Genesis 25:22–28?

5. What similarities or differences do you recognize between Jacob and Esau's rivalry and any rival relationship in your life right now?

6. What insights does the story of Jacob and Esau provide that might help you to diffuse any rivalries in your life?

Spend time prayerfully considering any rivalries in your own life. Ask God to bring reconciliation and peace to the relationship. Ask God to transform any areas of anger, unforgiveness, or angst into love for the other person.

DAY THREE: The Winning of the Birthright

GENESIS 25:29-34

The birthright is particularly valuable to the oldest son because it ensures a double portion of the family's estate. In ancient culture, a father's inheritance was divided evenly among all of the sons, except for the oldest, who received two portions. In a family with only two sons, the older son received everything. This probably became a point of contention for the twins Jacob and Esau, who were born moments apart.

Jacob negotiates a shrewd deal to steal his older brother's birthright. He desires the favored, privileged status of being the firstborn.

For Esau, his future inheritance is on the line. He's famished, and he must make a choice. Rather than refuse Jacob or negotiate the terms of the birthright, Esau reveals his impetuous, rash nature when he agrees to Jacob's outrageous terms. His quick response to Jacob also demonstrates that he doesn't value the birthright. Esau shows no remorse for what he's done. He simply eats, drinks, and goes on his way. Like Judas who denies Jesus for some cash, Esau sets the bar low when he denies his birthright for a hot meal.

NOTABLE
Jacob's name sounds like the word "cheat" in Hebrew.

1. Read Genesis 25:29–34. Use the following chart to list five adjectives each that describe Jacob and Esau.

JACOB	ESAU

NOTABLE

Jacob knows that with the birthright comes responsibility, the role of protecting and leading the family. But when you're the grandchild of Abraham, the birthright comes with something else: the promises of God. Remember, in Abraham's family, he who gets the birthright gets the covenant. This is high stakes!

2. Why do you think Jacob values the birthright more than Esau?

What in your own life do you tend to underappreciate but would greatly miss if it were gone?

NOTABLE

The theme of the younger displacing the older appears in other Bible stories, including Joseph and Judah, Moses and Aaron, and David and his older brothers.

3. Of the members of your family, whom do you struggle the most to get along with?

What efforts are you making now to strengthen that relationship?

4. Have you been able to accept the blessings and challenges of the family God has placed you in? Why or why not?

Spend some time praying for the members of your immediate and extended family. Ask God to bless, encourage, protect, and provide for your family. Invite him to show you what you can do to bring about reconciliation in any broken relationships.

DAY FOUR: A Family Torn Apart by Deception

GENESIS 26-27

It's been said, "Like father like son," but nowhere is this more apparent in Genesis than when Isaac encounters Abimelek.

1. Read Genesis 26. What elements of Isaac's story are similar to Abraham's?

Isaac knows that Jacob already has the birthright, but he believes he can still pass his blessing on to his favorite son, Esau. Isaac doesn't realize he has a savvy opponent—his wife. The couple is working against one another, maneuvering and manipulating to get the upper hand for what they want rather than what God wants.

2. Read Genesis 27:1–29. Rebekah presents a deplorable plan to trick Isaac into blessing Jacob instead of Esau. After hearing the plan, what is Jacob's primary concern (v. 12)?

What does this reveal about Jacob's character?

The blessing of the oldest son was meant to be a public event, but Isaac chooses to bless his son in private. On this important day, Isaac should be focused on celebrating the blessing, but instead he tries to keep the blessing a secret. Despite the importance of the occasion, Isaac is distracted by his appetite, as noted by repeated references to food, tasting food, and eating.

3. Read Genesis 27:30–46. How do Isaac and Esau respond to the news of the deception (vv. 33–34)?

Do you think Isaac and Esau's responses were appropriate? Why or why not?

QUOTABLE

"Jacob was on his way, a long meandering way, to becoming Israel."[14]

—H. Stephen Shoemaker

The woman who devised the scheme that caused Esau to hate Jacob must now devise a scheme to save Jacob's life. Rebekah sends Jacob to her homeland and promises to call for him when it's safe. Her favorite son won't return for twenty years.

4. In the previous Afterhours personal study, you were asked to make a list of five adjectives that described Jacob and Esau (page 98). How have you seen the descriptors of each man's character play out in Genesis 26–27?

BONUS ACTIVITY

Do you know a pastor, teacher, businessperson, coworker, parent, or leader who could use a kind word of hope and love? This week send a homemade card or handwritten letter. Give a gift card. Go out of your way to say thanks and encourage them to finish well.

5. Why do you think Isaac, whose life is marked by miraculous beginnings, reaches such a low point?

What lessons can you learn from Isaac's life on how to finish well?

6. What choices do you need to make now to ensure that you end well in your faith journey?

Spend some time asking God to show you any changes that you need to make in your own life today in order finish well. Ask God for the grace and strength to enact those changes for the long haul.

DAY FIVE: Jacob Encounters God

GENESIS 28

Esau is furious at Jacob for stealing both his birthright and blessing. Rebekah worries that if Jacob stays around the house any longer, Esau will kill him. Then, Esau will be punished and possibly killed as well, leaving her without either of her sons. To protect Jacob, Rebekah advises him to travel to Haran to stay with her brother Laban until Esau cools down. Before Jacob leaves, Isaac pulls him aside to bless him and to offer some specific instruction.

1. Read Genesis 28:1–9. What instructions and blessings does Isaac give Jacob?

What is significant about the instructions?

What is significant about the blessings?

Esau realizes that his choice of Canaanite wives displeases his father, so he goes to be with Ishmael near the border of Egypt and marries there. It's interesting to note that Ishmael was the rejected offspring of Abraham, and now the rejected son of Isaac goes to live among his descendants.

NOTABLE

The distance that Jacob traveled from Beersheba to Harran (Genesis 28:10) is approximately 550 miles and probably took Jacob more than a month.

2. Read Genesis 28:10–22. Jacob has an unforgettable dream. In the space below, draw a picture of the image Jacob saw in his dream. Why do you think God used this image to communicate to Jacob?

Has God ever used a dream to communicate to you? If so, how did the dream impact your faith?

3. Why do you think God took a different approach to pursuing Jacob than he used to pursue Abraham or Isaac?

Why do you think God takes different approaches to pursuing different people?

Prior to this encounter with God, Jacob has been recognized as a deceiver and swindler. Yet God still pursues Jacob, knowing he is a work in process.

God approaches Jacob at a vulnerable time. Jacob is a fugitive on the run from his brother and has traveled hundreds of miles from his family. He probably second-guesses himself daily, wondering if stealing Esau's birthright was really worth it. He may be looking over his shoulder frequently to see if his brother is pursuing him. Jacob certainly doesn't expect to meet God on his journey—so the encounter is unexpected, encouraging, and full of hope and life.

4. Jacob promises to give God a tithe of everything he receives. Why is this significant to the transformation taking place in Jacob's life?

What changes in your own heart and life have you seen when you've chosen to give financially or otherwise?

Spend some time prayerfully considering if there is anything of your time, talents, or resources that God is calling you to give. Respond to any nudges you sense from God to express his goodness and love through generosity to others.

It's Not about You

Genesis 28–36

Incomprehensible and immutable is the love of God. For it was not after we were reconciled to him by the blood of his Son that he began to love us, but he loved us before the foundation of the world, that with his only begotten Son we too might be sons of God before we were any thing at all.

— ST. AUGUSTINE OF HIPPO

God selected Abraham, a pagan, to become the forefather of the people of God. The Lord chose an infertile woman, Sarah, to give birth to the fulfillment of that divine promise. And now, God makes one of the most startling choices of all: He chooses Jacob to father the twelve tribes of Israel. This is a man who is convinced that it's all about him. Such self-centered thinking stands in opposition to the love God calls us to. Without the love of God infusing our lives, it is impossible to truly love others. God's love is the fuel for our love, and we burn brighter when we're filled up with the reality of that love.

GETTING STARTED: Select One (10-15 minutes)

Experiential Activity: Balderdash

What you'll need:

- The game of Balderdash

1. Spend 15–20 minutes playing a few rounds of Balderdash—a game in which you have to figure out who is telling the truth and choose whom to believe.
2. Discuss the following questions:
   - What do you think it was like to be Jacob's friend or family member knowing he was a master deceiver?
   - Do you find it relatively easy or difficult to deceive someone?
   - What kinds of people are the easiest for you to deceive? The hardest?
   - What situations are most likely to tempt you to deceive someone?
   - What is the outcome of a relationship that is founded on or tainted by deception?

Icebreaker Question

*If you're not doing the experiential activity, choose **one** of the following questions to begin your discussion.*

- Have you ever been new to an area or felt like an outsider and had someone reach out to you? Describe the experience. What did you learn through it?
- Describe a situation in the past three months in which you needed to be reminded, "It's not about you!"
- Make a list of things within our culture that contribute to the "it's all about me" mindset. How do you combat these things in your life?

VIDEO FIVE: It's Not about You (20 minutes)

As you watch the video, use the following outline to take notes on anything that stands out to you.

I felt like I was breathing in Jesus.

In ancient culture the blessing of the eldest son is an event people wanted to attend, but Isaac keeps it a secret. He plans to bless Esau where no one will hear or see.

On the run from Esau, the last thing Jacob expected to encounter was God.

As bad as we may want someone to believe, whether it's a family member, friend, or someone else, ultimately we are dependent on God working to bring people into a relationship with himself.

Israel—as a man and as a nation—emerges through the wrestling and wounding of God.

I sensed the conviction, the invitation of God's Spirit, to change my attitude and behavior.

GROUP DISCUSSION QUESTIONS (30–45 minutes)

1. Consider what you learned about God's love from the Afterhours personal studies or on the video. What caught your attention or stood out most to you?

2. Take turns reading Genesis 25:26–34 and 27:6–13. Where do you think Jacob got the idea that it was all about him?

Briefly describe how thinking "it's all about me" sometimes slips into the following areas of your life:

Work

Relationships

Daily life

NOTABLE

To learn more about Scum of the Earth, check out Mike Sares's book *Pure Scum: The Left-out, The Right-brained, and the Grace of God* (InterVarsity Press).

3. What disciplines, spiritual practices, or habits have you developed to help you think about others first?

The Birthright and the Blessing

4. Margaret observes, "Jacob, who believes that it's all about him, swindles his brother out of his birthright in exchange for soup and bread. But for Jacob, the birthright isn't enough." In what ways does self-centeredness promote greed?

What other sins do you become prone to when you embrace self-centered thinking and living?

BONUS ACTIVITY

Consider watching a fun film that explores the power and effects of deception. Movies such as *Ocean's Eleven* and *Catch Me If You Can* (both rated PG-13) are great conversation starters about what it means to be deceived and to deceive others.

God's Timeline

5. In Genesis 28, God reveals himself to Jacob, who then begins to undergo a transformation. Why do you think God didn't reveal himself to Jacob earlier—*before* Jacob swindled his brother and destroyed his family?

Who in your life do you wish God would reveal himself to faster? Explain.

6. What do you think God is trying to communicate to Jacob by revealing himself as "the God of your father Abraham and the God of Isaac" (Genesis 28:13)?

7. How does God's promise to Jacob in Genesis 28:14 compare to God's promise to Abraham in Genesis 22:17? What does the commitment—to stay with a man who has been a deceptive swindler—reveal about God's love and faithfulness?

NOTABLE

In ancient times, olive oil was poured on objects to dedicate them to God. The process of pouring the oil is known as "anointing."

Jacob experiences the fear of the Lord. He responds in awe and wonder at what has just happened. In order to commemorate the moment, Jacob sets up a pillar and pours oil over it to consecrate it. He names the place Bethel, meaning "house of God." Then Jacob makes a vow to God, a vow which reveals a reorientation in Jacob's life. Jacob makes the commitment to God on the condition that the Lord's presence, protection, and provision remain with him.

Encountering God

8. In Genesis 27:20, Jacob describes God as "your God," but in Genesis 28:20–22 Jacob refers to God as "my God." Why is it important for Jacob's faith to become his own?

When would you say your faith became your own? What circumstances or relationships helped to make it possible?

Encounters with God are unexpected and often transform us. Sometimes they expose our weakness and leave us limping. Yet they invite us into a deeper relationship with God.

9. When in the last three months have you had an encounter with God? How did the experience affect your perspective of God, yourself, or life?

10. Briefly describe a difficulty you are facing in *one* of the following areas:

Your life overall

Your workplace or daily life

Your relationships (family or friends)

Your spiritual life

How might God be using this situation, as he did with Jacob, to cause you to grow, to recognize it's not about you, and to experience his transforming power?

The story of Jacob is a powerful reminder that no one is beyond the reach of God's transforming power. Though our culture cries, "It's all about you," the Spirit steadily reminds us that it's all about God. When we reorient ourselves, our lives, our everything in a Godward direction, we can't help but experience spiritual transformation.

CLOSE IN PRAYER

Ask God to:

- Shift your thinking from self-focused to others-focused.
- Provide opportunities for you to serve and give.
- Help you become a more vibrant conduit of God's love and blessing.

JUMPSTART

To prepare for the next group session, read Genesis 36–50 and tackle the Afterhours personal studies.

Afterhours Personal Studies

Dive deeper into the book of Genesis by engaging in these five personal studies. If you only have time for one, choose Day Five, which will prepare you specifically for the next session.

DAY ONE: Jacob Falls Head over Heels in Love

GENESIS 29:1-30

While traveling toward Harran, Jacob stops for the night and uses a stone for a pillow (Genesis 28:11). That evening he has an unforgettable dream and encounter with God that changes the course of his life. Now Jacob is about to encounter another stone, a much larger one, which will again change his destiny.

1. Read Genesis 29:1–30. What do you think compels Jacob to remove the stone from the well?

What does Jacob's action reveal about his character and who he has become?

NOTABLE

Stones were placed on top of wells to prevent evaporation, for sanitary reasons—to keep them clean and protect them from wild animals—as well as to prevent people from accidentally falling in.

2. What is Jacob's response to Rachel (Genesis 29:11)?

Why do you think Jacob weeps?

3. What attracts Laban's attention to Abraham's servant in Genesis 24:30?

What attracts Laban's attention to Jacob in Genesis 29:13?

What does this foreshadow about Laban's character?

Laban expects Jacob to work for him for free because he is a family member, but Jacob negotiates with him. Jacob agrees to work for seven years, reducing his status from family member to hired helper in exchange for marrying Laban's younger daughter, Rachel.

NOTABLE

Leah's name means "cow" while Rachel's name means "ewe." Both names are appropriate for a family living in an agrarian world caring for sheep. Yet Laban treats his daughters like barnyard animals that are bartered and sold.

4. Laban pretends to be outraged that Jacob wants to take the younger daughter before the older. How does Jacob reap what he sows in his relationship with Laban?

5. Read Galatians 6:7–8. When have you seen the principle of reaping and sowing revealed in your own life?

Spend some time asking God for wisdom on where you can sow better seed in your life and the lives of others. Ask God to help you to recognize the principle of sowing and reaping in your own life.

DAY TWO: The Battle of the Brides

GENESIS 29:31–30:43

Leah is described as not being loved. The Hebrew word used here actually means "to be hated." She's rejected and despised but, because of Jacob's agreement with Laban, he cannot divorce her. One can only imagine the loneliness and heartache Leah feels. Yet God sees her pain and loss.

1. Read Genesis 29:31–35. In the following chart, match each of the four sons born to Leah in this passage to the meaning of their names.

NAME	HEBREW MEANING
Reuben	The LORD has heard
Simeon	I will praise the LORD
Levi	See, a son! The LORD has seen my misery
Judah	My husband will be attached to me

The names of Leah's sons reveal much about her own journey. Leah is in awe that God opens her womb and gives her a child. She knows God has seen her anguish and misery. Then Leah recognizes God's providence and provision in the birth of her second son, though she is still unloved. With the third son, Leah is hopeful that she will win over the heart of Jacob. With the birth of her fourth son, Judah, Leah comes to terms with her lot in life and offers praise to God.

NOTABLE

Levi becomes the ancestor of Aaron, whose descendants become the priests of Israel. One of Judah's descendants becomes King David whose descendants trace to the Messiah. God uses the lineage of an unloved daughter to give birth to Jesus.

Each of Leah's four sons must arouse jealousy in Rachel. As much as Rachel wants to have a child, she is barren. The two sisters enter into a fierce competition to see who can have the most children.

2. Read Genesis 30:1–24. In what ways do Rachel and Leah each want what the other sister has been given?

Do you tend to focus more on what you have or what you don't have?

What is the result?

QUOTABLE

"The atmosphere in the household was electric with tension and jealousy as the two sisters crowed triumphantly over each other as each successive son was born."[15]

—Karen Armstrong

Rachel doesn't seem to appreciate the fact that she is loved by Jacob, and Leah doesn't seem to appreciate the fact that she has children. The sisters both reach a point where they're more focused on what they don't have than what they've been given.

In their struggle to win Jacob's love—and the social status that comes with bearing children—Rachel and Leah turn to their maids. At one point, the two women actually negotiate who will spend an evening with Jacob by bargaining with a plant called a mandrake. Leah's son Reuben discovers some mandrakes in a field and brings them to Leah. When Rachel catches sight of the mandrakes, she wants what her sister has. She offers Jacob to Leah for the evening in exchange for the love fruits. That evening, Leah conceives Issachar, whose name means, "God has rewarded me."

Despite Jacob's prayerlessness, Rachel's bitterness, and Leah's rivalry, God still blesses the family with a dozen sons and a daughter named Dinah, reminding us that God's grace and goodness extend beyond our selfishness and sin.

3. Use the following chart to identify key information about the twelve sons and one daughter of Jacob, including their birth order and the meaning of their names. Some answers are provided, so use the clues on the chart to fill in *all* the remaining blanks.

SCRIPTURE	LEAH'S CHILDREN	MEANING OF NAME	BIRTH ORDER
Genesis 29:32		See, a son!	
	Simeon		
Genesis 29:34			
			4
Genesis 30:17–18			
		Honor	
Genesis 30:21		*Meaning not given*	11
SCRIPTURE	**ZILPAH'S SONS (LEAH'S MAID)**	**MEANING OF NAME**	**BIRTH ORDER**
	Gad		
Genesis 30:12–15		Happy	
SCRIPTURE	**RACHEL'S SONS**	**MEANING OF NAME**	**BIRTH ORDER**
Genesis 30:22–24			12
Genesis 35:16–18		Happy	13
SCRIPTURE	**BILHAH'S SONS (RACHEL'S MAID)**	**MEANING OF NAME**	**BIRTH ORDER**
	Dan		
Genesis 30:7–8		My struggle	

4. Rachel and her maid have four children while Leah and her maid have nine. What comfort do you find in knowing that God champions the needs of the weak and unloved?

5. Read Genesis 30:25–43. Who do you think acted more shrewdly—Laban or Jacob? Why?

6. Does it surprise you that God uses such a dysfunctional family to give birth to the twelve tribes of Israel? Why or why not?

What hope does this story provide for you that God can use anything and anyone?

Spend some time thanking God for the ways he can redeem even the most broken and messed-up situations. Thank God for the ways your own areas of pain, brokenness, and dysfunction have been healed and redeemed as testimonies of his goodness and faithfulness.

DAY THREE: A Divine Encounter

GENESIS 31–32

Jacob and Laban's relationship deteriorates to the point of outright hostilities. God directs Jacob to return to Canaan. Upon hearing the news, Rachel and Leah choose to give up their own family in favor of staying with Jacob, which is a stinging blow to Laban. The shrewd father-in-law chases Jacob down and accuses him of stealing an idol.

1. Read Genesis 31:1–42. In what ways has God used the twenty years of hardship serving under Laban to transform Jacob?

How have times of hardship transformed you spiritually?

NOTABLE

A portion of the amount of money given for marriage is meant to go to the daughter. In other words, some of the wages Jacob worked fourteen years to earn belong to Rachel and Leah.

2. What do you think compels the women to leave their homeland to go with Jacob?

3. Why do you think Rachel commits the crime of "godnapping" by stealing idols from her father's household?

Why is it so important that the idols not be found?

4. Read Genesis 31:43–55. In what ways is this scene proof that Laban and Jacob can't agree on anything?

How do you navigate a relationship in which you can't seem to agree on anything?

Going home means Jacob will have to face his brother Esau. Just as Jacob encountered God after his fallout with Esau, he now encounters God before the reconciliation with his brother.

5. Read Genesis 32. What steps does Jacob take to prepare for the meeting with his brother?

How do you prepare for a meeting in which you want to mend a relationship?

Jacob's encounter with God reveals that there's something unexpected and ambiguous about a divine encounter. Divine encounters don't happen on our terms, but God's terms. They surprise us. They often happen at our low points. They remind us of our own weakness. They invite us into deeper relationship with God. Just as Jacob's encounter with God didn't equate to ease and comfort, often ours don't either. Divine encounters remind us that God is fully in control and we are not. Although every encounter with God has a uniquely mysterious element to it, the hallmark of every divine encounter is that we walk (or limp) away as different people.

QUOTABLE

"Many of us, like Jacob, have wrestled with something, for something, without really knowing what we sought. Jacob, having now finally gotten ahold of God, finds what he was seeking, and refuses to let go."[16]

—John C. L. Gibson

6. Jacob meets God at night. In the morning, he's a different person. Jacob is now Israel. Have you ever had a situation in which you limped away a better person? Describe.

Spend some time prayerfully reflecting on God-encounter moments in the past when you limped away a better person. Thank God for the opportunities and encounters he has used to grow your faith and transform you into who you are today.

DAY FOUR: Esau, Dinah, and Israel

GENESIS 33–36

The challenges Jacob faces stretch his faith, expose his heart, and force him to grow. When Esau meets Jacob for the first time after many years, both men have changed in countless ways.

1. Read Genesis 33. Jacob wrestles God at night and is reunited with his brother later that same day. What do you think surprises Israel most about the encounter?

What do you think surprises Esau most about the encounter?

Following Jacob's reconciliation, a powerful scene unfolds with Jacob's only daughter, Dinah. While living in Canaan, Dinah is raped by prince Shechem. Jacob's sons confront the wrongdoing with violence.

2. Why do you think it's significant that Jacob settles in sight of the city in Genesis 33:18? How did this endanger Dinah?

3. Read Genesis 34. What does the story reveal about Jacob's family?

God continues pursuing a relationship with Jacob (Israel). God calls Jacob to Bethel to build an altar. In response, Jacob purges his household of false gods and asks everyone in his household to cleanse themselves and change their clothes as a symbol that they are living a new and purified way of life. After cleansing his home of idols, Jacob and his family make their way to Bethel. Bethel marks a shift in the life of Jacob.

After God reaffirms the promises to Jacob at Bethel, Rachel dies giving birth to Benjamin. This marks both an end and a beginning for Jacob. The focus of Jacob's story shifts from his wives to his sons.

4. Read Genesis 35. How does Reuben, the oldest son, disqualify himself from ruling over the twelve tribes of Israel (v. 22)?

When have you been tempted to do something that would disqualify you from leadership?

How did you handle the situation?

5. Read Genesis 36, which offers the genealogy of Esau in Canaan as well as his separation from Canaan. Why do you think Esau's genealogy begins with him taking wives from the daughters of Canaan?

What does this reveal about Esau?

Why do you think the death of Esau isn't reported?

Is your own spiritual journey more reflective of Esau or Jacob? Explain.

The twelve tribes of Esau and the land of Edom reflect Esau's choices. Like Ishmael, Esau cuts himself off from the line of blessing by marrying Canaanite wives. Like Lot, he leaves the Promised Land for lands that offer greater prosperity. Despite Esau's poor choices, his descendants benefit from God's faithfulness. Edom becomes a great nation—one that prospers and grows. Deuteronomy 23:7 challenges, "Do not abhor an Edomite, for he is your brother." Yet despite its growth, Edom can never compare to Israel. The older brother will always serve the younger.

6. Read Genesis 37. What surprises you about the initial portrait of Joseph?

In what ways is Joseph like Jacob?

Spend some time prayerfully reflecting on the life of Jacob. Ask God to reveal which lessons from Jacob's life apply to your own life right now.

DAY FIVE: Selling a Dreamer into Slavery

GENESIS 37

Following the genealogy of Esau, Genesis 37 begins by noting that Jacob lived in the land of Canaan. This stands in stark contrast to Esau who lived in the hill country of Seir (Genesis 36:9). The mention highlights the choice made by Jacob to remain in the Promised Land.

Now we're introduced to the story of Joseph, the youngest son of Jacob and Rachel, until Benjamin is born later. Just as Esau was Isaac's favorite son, Joseph is Jacob's favorite. The favoritism ignites rivalry among the twelve sons of Jacob.

1. Read Genesis 37. Based on this account of Joseph's actions, list six to eight words you would use to describe Joseph.

Which of the words you listed might also be used to describe yourself as a teenager?

2. Complete the following chart to identify the actions that cause tension between Joseph and his brothers.

SCRIPTURE	ACTIONS THAT CAUSE TENSION
Genesis 37:2	
Genesis 37:3–4	
Genesis 37:5–11	

Reflecting on the chart, do you think the brothers' response to Joseph is justified or unjustified (Genesis 37:19–20)? Why or why not?

3. How do you typically respond when you are provoked by someone?

4. Recognizing that the rape at Shechem (Genesis 34) occurred only two years earlier when Joseph was fifteen, do you think Jacob is wise to send his Joseph to Shechem (Genesis 37:13)? Why or why not?

What does Jacob's decision reveal about him?

NOTABLE

Twenty shekels of silver was equivalent to approximately five years' wages for a shepherd.

5. Not only do Joseph's brothers want to kill Joseph's dreams, but they want to kill the dreamer. Have you ever had your dreams intentionally squashed by someone else? If so, how did you respond?

Have you ever been the one to squash someone else's dreams? If so, how did you feel afterward?

6. How have you responded to the opposition or struggle in your own life as you've sought to fulfill a God-given dream?

Spend some time asking God to reignite any snuffed dreams in your life. Ask God to reveal ways for you to be a source of encouragement for other people's dreams.

Finding God among Prisons and Palaces

Genesis 37–50

He who counts the stars and calls them by their names is in no danger of forgetting His own children. He knows your case as thoroughly as if you were the only creature He ever made, or the only saint He ever loved.

—C. H. SPURGEON

In the midst of difficult circumstances, we sometimes wonder, "Where is God?" Yet the story of Joseph reveals that no matter what our emotions or circumstances may try to tell us, God is still present and faithful to the promises he has made.

Joseph's story reveals that even though we cannot control circumstances, we can control how we respond to those circumstances. Joseph spent many years in prison and suffered multiple injustices, yet God continued to pursue Joseph and displays a divine plan for the people through Joseph's unexpected rise to power.

GETTING STARTED: Select One (10 - 15 minutes)

Experiential Activity: From Prison to President

What you'll need:

- Information on Nelson Mandela from your local library or online

1. Spend some time researching the life story of Nelson Mandela, a modern leader who spent time both in prisons and palaces.
2. Highlight a few facts about Mandela and consider showing any clips from YouTube or a video about Mandela's life.
3. Discuss the parallels between Nelson Mandela and Joseph.
   - What common emotions do you think they felt?
   - What fears do you think they both experienced?
   - What doubts do you think they both shared about their futures?

Icebreaker Question

*If you're not doing the experiential activity, choose **one** of the following questions to begin your discussion.*

- Sometimes life doesn't turn out like we expect. What unexpected surprises has life given you?
- What types of situations make you wonder, "Where are you, God?"
- Have you ever had an experience in which someone intended evil or harm but God used it for good? If so, describe.

VIDEO SIX: Finding God among
Prisons and Palaces (19 minutes)

As you watch the video, use the following outline to take notes on anything that stands out to you.

Sometimes life doesn't turn out like you expect.

With jealousy brewing, Joseph should keep a low profile. But it's almost as if he can't help himself.

Life isn't turning out how Joseph expects. On the long caravan ride to Egypt I have a hunch Joseph asked the question, "Where are you, God?"

God uses the most unlikely set of circumstances to preserve and prosper not just Joseph, but his people.

Years before, Joseph's two dreams got him into a dungeon; now, interpreting these two dreams will get him out.

God is present both in the palaces and in the prisons, in the years of feast and the years of famine.

GROUP DISCUSSION QUESTIONS (30–45 minutes)

1. Consider what you learned about God's love and faithfulness from the Afterhours personal studies or on the video. What caught your attention or stood out most to you?

The Dreamer

2. Joseph has been given a tremendous gift for dream interpretation, but the way he handles his gift almost gets him killed. How have you seen spiritual gifts misused or abused? What makes the difference?

NOTABLE
Joseph's dreams are the first dreams in the Bible in which God does not speak. The dreams described throughout Joseph's story always come in pairs.

3. Joseph finds great favor with Potiphar, only to be falsely accused and then imprisoned. Joseph rises to favor with the jailer and interprets the dreams of fellow prisoners, only to be forgotten. At some point in life, we all experience some kind of injustice. How do you respond to the times when life isn't fair?

What does the story of Joseph reveal about how to handle these experiences?

Where Is God?

4. Are there any situations in your own life right now where you're wondering, "Where are you, God?" If so, describe.

5. Why do you think the promises of God often require years of waiting and hardship?

How has waiting and hardship shaped your own spiritual growth and character?

When have you experienced God as "I AM"?

6. What do the following passages reveal about what waiting on God through hardship produces in our lives?

Romans 5:3

1 Peter 2:20–23

Do you tend to run toward or away from hardship? Explain.

Every Step of the Way

7. In our faith journeys, we encounter times when we need to move forward and take risks and other times when we need to wait patiently and pray. How do you discern when you're supposed to move forward and when you're supposed to wait?

NOTABLE

Joseph's dream in Genesis 37:7 of his brothers (represented by the sheaves) bowing down is fulfilled in progressive stages. His brothers bow once in Genesis 42:6, twice in Genesis 43:26, 28, and then throw themselves at his feet in Genesis 50:18.

8. When Joseph encounters his brothers, he tests them multiple times before revealing himself to them. Why do you think Joseph tests them?

Have you ever tested anyone to see if they've changed or been transformed? If so, describe.

9. The original temptation of Adam and Eve in the garden circled around the question of whether or not God really loves us. In other words, is God good and loving and can God be trusted? In what ways have you discovered that God is loving and good and faithful as you've studied the book of Genesis?

NOTABLE

Joseph lives both the first and the last seventeen years of his life with Jacob (Genesis 37:2; 47:28), signifying the perfect timing of God in his life.

10. Reflecting on your study here in Genesis of pursuing God's love, how would you describe what it means to serve the God of Abraham, Isaac, and Jacob?

Why is it important to pursue God's love in your own life?

The story of Joseph is a powerful reminder that even when things don't make sense, God is still at work. When we wonder, "Where are you, God?" we can trust that God is more involved than we can ever imagine.

CLOSE IN PRAYER

Ask God to:
- Continue revealing his presence and guidance in your life.
- Provide opportunities to use the unique gifts you've been given.
- Give you courage to walk faithfully into all he has for you.

JUMPSTART

Tackle the Afterhours personal studies and consider organizing a "midterm" gathering to connect, share a meal, and hang out with your group. Next up: six sessions based on the Gospel of John, "Pursuing God's Love."

BONUS ACTIVITY

If Andrew Lloyd Webber's *Joseph and the Amazing Technicolor Dreamcoat* is being staged in your area, consider gathering a group of friends to attend the performance. Or consider streaming it or renting a video. Reflect on how the play follows the biblical story and where the story heads in a different direction.

SESSION SIX

Afterhours Personal Studies

Dive deeper into the book of Genesis by engaging in these five personal studies.

DAY ONE: Unlikely Faith

GENESIS 38

If the rivalry among Jacob's sons with Joseph wasn't enough, we're now given a glimpse into another of Jacob's sons, Judah. He leaves his family in order to take up residence among the Canaanites and ends up marrying a Canaanite woman. Together they have had three sons: Er, Onan, and Shelah. Judah selects a woman named Tamar to marry his oldest son, Er. The Scripture notes that because Er was evil, God took his life. This is the first time in Scripture that explicitly says God put someone to death.

Er's death leaves Tamar in a predicament. According to the law of the time, the brother of the deceased is responsible to marry the widow and raise up a son in the brother's name. Thus, Judah's second son, Onan, is required to marry Tamar and have children. Although he proceeds to marry Tamar, Onan knows any children won't be his and so he ensures she doesn't become pregnant. God takes Onan's life, too.

NOTABLE
The name Er in Hebrew is known to spell "evil" backward.

Both of Tamar's husbands have died. The last thing Judah wants is for his third son to experience a similar fate. Instead of marrying her to Shelah, he sends the widow away to live with her father. Rather than marry a Canaanite husband, she remains true to Judah's family in a daring act of faith and becomes the heroine of the story.

1. Read Genesis 38. While Genesis 37 offers a detailed look at the character of Joseph, Genesis 38 provides a detailed look at the character of Judah. What similarities and differences do you note between the two?

2. In ancient culture, women fulfilled one of two major roles. Either they married and produced children for their husband, or they were unmarried and remained virgins in their father's home. With Er's death, Tamar is left in a precarious situation as a barren widow. Why is Judah's response to Tamar wicked?

Tamar knows Judah had no intention to give her his third son, Shelah, in marriage. She plots to outsmart Judah by matching deception with deception. Tamar may have been familiar with ancient laws that suggest that if a married man and his brothers all died, the father is responsible for her. Judah unwittingly hires Tamar as a prostitute. As a promise of payment for her services, she asks for his signet ring, cord, and staff. In modern terms, this would be like asking for a man's wallet with his identification, credit cards, and social security card tucked inside.

When Judah wakes up the next day he realizes he's made a foolish mistake and asks his friend Hirah to retrieve his possessions and pay the woman.

NOTABLE

Four women are mentioned in the genealogy of Jesus in the Gospel of Matthew. All of the women—Tamar, Rahab, Ruth, and Bathsheba—are outsiders to Israel and their marriages are marked by scandal, yet God notes their faith and deems them worthy.

3. Reflecting on Genesis 38:15–24, do you think Judah has more concern for Tamar as the prostitute or as his daughter-in-law?

When Judah discovers what he's done, he takes responsibility for Tamar and acknowledges her righteousness. Judah honors Tamar as a bride. Though Judah's two sons had died, Tamar gives birth to two more sons—Perez and Zerah—who will carry on the family name. The sons' names can be translated "bursting forth" (Perez) and "shining forth" (Zerah). The names reflect Perez's bursting forth to become the firstborn and the favor that reflected on Judah as Zerah and his brother were born.

4. Would you describe Tamar as a victim or an overcomer? Explain.

Reflecting on your own life, would you describe yourself more as a victim or an overcomer?

QUOTABLE

"It may seem a bit strange to put the word 'redeemer' with Tamar, but in the Hebrew scripture the word 'redeemer' means 'to take responsibility for' and refers to persons who take responsibility for others and who call people to responsibility. A redeemer, then, is one who keeps life and love alive, who sees people do right by each other, and who keeps the family going and the community intact."[17]

—H. Stephen Shoemaker

5. What signs of transformation appear in Judah's life (Genesis 38:26)?

How is God honored when you take responsibility for your actions?

God promises Perez's offspring will not only be plentiful but royal. Judah is selected as the carrier of royal lineage, despite having evil sons. Because of Tamar's faithfulness, this promise is fulfilled. Ten generations separate King David from Perez (Ruth 4:18–22). Thus, Perez's emergence ahead of his brother is significant and places him in the line of the Messiah.

Spend some time prayerfully considering if there are any areas of your life in which you've failed to take responsibility. Ask God to give you the courage and strength to walk in integrity and do the right thing.

DAY TWO: Highs and Lows of Joseph's Journey

GENESIS 39–41

After being sold into slavery, Joseph finds favor with his master and he's eventually appointed head of the entire household. Then Potiphar's wife makes a sexual advance toward Joseph. When Joseph rejects her, she falsely accuses him of impropriety and he's sent to prison.

1. Read Genesis 39. Why is it significant that the author of Genesis notes that the Lord was with Joseph (Genesis 39:2, 21)?

What types of situations tend to challenge your belief that God is with you?

2. Judah faces sexual temptation in Genesis 38 and now Joseph faces sexual temptation in Genesis 39. How does each respond and what is the result?

When are you most likely to experience sexual temptation in your own life?

What helpful habits or practices do you use to resist sexual temptation?

While in prison, Joseph finds favor with the prison warden who shows him kindness or *hesed*, the Hebrew word meaning to act with love and loyalty (Genesis 39:21). Two other servants are thrown in prison: the king's cupbearer and the king's cook. Each has an unusual dream, which Joseph interprets.

QUOTABLE

"The ingratitude of the Egyptian cupbearer prefigures the later national experience of the Israelites in Egypt (Exodus 1:8)."[18]

—Nahum M. Sarna

3. Read Genesis 40. Do you think the cupbearer's forgetfulness of what Joseph has done for him is due to a mental or a moral lapse or something else? Explain.

What does the forgetfulness reveal about the cupbearer?

Is there anyone in your life that you've forgotten who, like the cupbearer, you need to remember and show thanks to?

BONUS ACTIVITY
Who has invested extra time in your life? Take time to write notes or make calls to express gratitude.

Two years after the cupbearer's life was spared, the king of Egypt has two dreams that beg interpretation. The cupbearer finally remembers Joseph. Joseph interprets the king's dreams and then is made the governor over Egypt.

4. Read Genesis 41. Joseph's gift of dream interpretation suggests he has access to a higher power and authority than the Pharaoh of Egypt. What does Joseph's gift of dream interpretation reveal about God?

How does Joseph acknowledge God in his dream interpretations (Genesis 41:16, 25, 28)?

Overall, do you find yourself quick or slow to ascribe thanks to God when he works in your life? Place an X on the continuum to indicate your response.

I am slow to give thanks.   I am quick to give thanks.

5. God doesn't just give Joseph the dream of his brothers bowing down to him once, but twice. Often when God speaks to us, the louder the message, the more difficult the journey. In what ways have you found this to be true in your own life?

Spend some time reflecting on the highs and lows of your own faith journey. Thank God for loving you and pursuing you every step of the way.

DAY THREE: When Dreams Come True

GENESIS 42-45

Pharaoh acknowledges that the Spirit of God is with Joseph. The Hebrew word for Spirit is *ruah* and can be translated "wind." The same word, *ruah*, is used in the creation story in Genesis 1:2 when it speaks of the Spirit hovering over the waters. After more than a dozen years of unjust treatment, Joseph is placed in the second position of power in all of Egypt. When the seven years of plenty that Joseph predicted come to an end, famine strikes the land. Jacob and his sons are afflicted. Ten of Joseph's brothers travel to Egypt to buy grain.

1. Read Genesis 42. Why do you think Joseph chooses not to reveal himself to his brothers?

2. What signs of transformation do you see in Jacob's sons in Genesis 42?

3. Read Genesis 43. The servant tells the brothers *shalom*, meaning "peace," or what we might describe as "it's all right" when they describe the silver found in the grain sacks. In what ways is *shalom* or peace restored among the brothers in Genesis 43?

4. Read Genesis 44–45. Why is the brothers' response, in particular that of Judah (Genesis 44), so important for the family reconciliation that takes place in Genesis 45?

5. Joseph reveals his identity to his brothers. He reassures them that he harbors no desire for revenge and that God has used what they meant for harm to accomplish good. What do the following passages reveal about the idea that God is working to bring about what is good?

    Proverbs 16:1–4

Proverbs 20:24

Proverbs 27:1

6. At first glance, portions of Joseph's story seem to be attributed to "happenstance" but turn out to be "divine circumstance." Do you tend to attribute the events in your life more to happenstance or to divine circumstance?

How does your perspective affect your personal journey with God?

Spend some time reflecting on the challenges you're facing in life right now. Ask God to give you a divine perspective on situations and circumstances that he wants to use to glorify himself.

DAY FOUR: The End of the Beginning

GENESIS 46–50

The reuniting of Jacob and Joseph is a powerful moment of family reconciliation and joy. After his family's arrival, Joseph carefully negotiates the land of Goshen for his family.

Goshen is the best of the land, ideal for grazing animals. Since shepherding is a profession despised by Egyptians, relocating to Goshen also protects Joseph's family by keeping them separate from the Egyptians. The request also signifies to Pharaoh that the Israelites don't have a political agenda and aren't a threat. On this land the Israelites prosper and multiply.

1. Read Genesis 46–48. Why do you think God reassures Jacob of his promises?

When in your spiritual journey do you most need to be reminded of God's promises?

 NOTABLE
Genesis 47 tells the story of a Hebrew making slaves of the Egyptians. The first chapter of Exodus tells the story of Egyptians making slaves of the Hebrews.

2. Under Joseph's leadership, the Egyptians become slaves. According to the following passages, what do the people give and receive in exchange?

Genesis 47:14

Genesis 47:16

Genesis 47:19–20

What kinds of things do you tend to become enslaved to without realizing that it's happening?

NOTABLE

Genesis concludes with Joseph's request to have his bones carried back to his home. Four centuries later, this oath is remembered, fulfilled, and confirmed by Joshua (Joshua 24:32).

3. Read Genesis 49–50. Upon their father's death, how do Joseph's brothers try to protect themselves (50:15–18)?

What is Joseph's response (50:19–21)?

What does this reveal about Joseph's character?

What opportunities has God been giving you recently to refine your character?

4. Though embalmed in Egypt, Jacob is buried in the Promised Land (Genesis 50:4–14). Why is this significant to the promise God gave to Abraham many years before (Genesis 12:1–3)?

What does Jacob's burial in the Promised Land reveal about God's love, pursuit of humankind, and faithfulness?

Spend some time reflecting on the ways God has displayed faithfulness to you over the last decade. Thank God for his presence and persistence in your life.

BONUS ACTIVITY

Now that you've read and studied six stories from Genesis, take some time to create a short outline of the book of Genesis. This can be as simple as outlining the general chapters in which major stories are told. After you develop your outline, take time committing the outline to memory. That way when you need to find a story from Genesis quickly in your Bible, you'll have a good idea of where to turn!

DAY FIVE: Reflecting on the Love of God in Genesis

After engaging in a Bible study, sometimes it's easy to move on to the next one without taking time to reflect on what God has been communicating to you. Like a traveler on a long road trip, you can wake up and wonder, "Where have I just been?"

1. Spend a few moments flipping through the pages of sessions one through six. Which statements or notes did you underline or highlight?

    Why were these meaningful to you?

2. What did you learn through this study that you'd never known before about the book of Genesis?

    How do these insights impact your relationship with Jesus?

3. Why is it important to continue pursuing God's love in your own life? What practical steps can you take to do so?

4. Where have you seen God's love most clearly displayed in Genesis?

5. One of the foundational truths of Genesis traces back to the opening words, "In the beginning God." In what ways has your own faith in God been strengthened through this study?

Spend time thanking God for all that you've learned through this study about his love and presence in our world. Ask God for the grace not only to experience his love but also to reflect it in your everyday life.

PURSUING GOD'S BEAUTY

Beauty has a way of stopping us in our tracks. When we encounter something that's truly beautiful, we can't help but pause for a moment.

I've seen beautiful expressions, such as the lingering nuances of the setting sun, cause people to pause, watch, and reflect as they drink in the scene. Indeed, beauty has a way of gripping our hearts and refusing to let go.

Why pursue God's beauty?

Because the beauty of God radiates in the person of Jesus Christ—the person in whom God placed his whole heart on display for the world to see.

The Gospel of John is a book whose beauty invites us to stop in our tracks, not just because it's beautifully written, but because of the stunning portraits of Jesus found throughout. The twenty-one chapters of John tell stories of Jesus walking into people's lives and transforming them forever. Jesus knows no boundaries. The Son of God enters the lives of fishermen and centurions, the physically and spiritually blind, as well as a wide range of religious leaders and religious rejects, inviting them all to believe. Those who accept the invitation find their lives forever changed.

Despite the overwhelming presence of God's beauty, some are tempted to dismiss beauty as merely subjective because aesthetic opinions differ. Others dismiss beauty as deceptive because some have perverted beauty into unmentionables. Still others turn away from beauty because it's not essential or functional.

Yet God is the one who fills all of creation with beauty. God strings galaxies in the sky and submerges creatures in the depths of the sea—some of which have yet to be discovered. Indeed, the heavens and earth declare the glory of God. The stories found in John are ones we need to study and be reminded of because they beckon us to love God even more.

My hope and prayer is that through the final six sessions you'll be reminded of the work of God in your life and share that beautiful news with others.

Encountering Jesus

John 1–3

Each one of us has different experiences of God's beauty and different appre-
ciations of this beauty—those inexpressible and indefinable moments that
deeply touch our hearts, our minds, and all our senses. Those moments that
melt our hearts when we feel the presence of God in what is beautiful. Each
one of us will tell different stories of when we have heard beauty, seen beauty,
smelled beauty, tasted beauty and touched beauty . . . when beauty has touched
our inner souls, when God has touched us.[19]

—EDWARD F. MARKQUART

Throughout the Gospel of John, the beauty of God radiates in the person of Jesus Christ—a person in whom God placed his whole heart on display for the world to see. It's within the person of Jesus that we find the invisible attributes of God being made visible, on display like the fine pieces of artwork in a gallery—to be enjoyed, celebrated, and reflected upon.

If we are going to be people who pursue God's beauty, who live passionately pursuing Jesus Christ, then we cannot keep the stories of what God has been doing in our lives to ourselves. Each of us is a mini-portrait of the beautiful work of God. As recipients of God's grace and love, we have the opportunity to display the beauty of God everywhere we go simply by sharing the story of God's work in our lives.

Wherever we may be on our spiritual journeys, there's something powerful and beautiful we can discover from each other's stories of meeting Jesus. Every story showcases facets of God's goodness and demonstrates how relentlessly God pursues us.

GETTING STARTED: Select One (10–15 minutes)

Experiential Activity: When Love Comes to Town

What you'll need:

- An MP3 of U2's "When Love Comes to Town"
- Printed lyrics of U2's "When Love Comes to Town" for each participant

1. Download "When Love Comes to Town."
2. Google the lyrics and print them out for each participant.
3. Play the song and allow participants to read through the lyrics.
4. Discuss the following questions:
    - What images and messages are suggested through the song?
    - What does it look like in your own life when love comes to town?
    - Have you ever seen love come to town in someone else's life? What did it look like? How were they transformed? How were you impacted from seeing the transformation?

Icebreaker Question

*If you're not doing the experiential activity, choose **one** of the following sets of questions to begin your discussion.*

- Where did you see beauty this week? How did it impact your relationship with God?
- Have you ever met someone famous? Describe the experience.
- Imagine for a moment that you had the opportunity to meet Jesus tomorrow for breakfast at a local restaurant. Where would you eat together? What would you order? What questions would you ask?

VIDEO SEVEN: Encountering Jesus (18 minutes)

As you watch the video, use the following outline to take notes on anything that stands out to you.

We all have different stories, unique portraits of the ways we first encountered Jesus.

At times, we will simply declare the truth of who Jesus is, and those who hear will become followers of Jesus.

We need to bring people to Jesus. What does that mean? We need to recognize that bringing people to Jesus is a journey in which we share our faith and our lives.

Sometimes when it comes to helping people encounter Jesus, all we can do is invite them to "come and see."

Sometimes people will have encounters with God that are miraculous, mysterious, beyond human explanation, but essential for their decision to follow Jesus.

If we are going to be people who pursue God's beauty, people who want to see our magnificent God on display everywhere we go, then we cannot keep the stories of what God has been doing in our lives to ourselves.

GROUP DISCUSSION QUESTIONS (30–45 minutes)

1. What caught your attention or stood out most to you on the video?

Encountering Jesus

2. How did you first encounter Jesus? Where were you? Who were you with? What series of circumstances led to that encounter?

3. Jesus' approach to calling his disciples was revolutionary. Traditionally, disciples made the choice of which rabbi they would follow. But Jesus does the opposite. Instead of waiting for the disciples to find him, Jesus takes the initiative and pursues his followers. Read John 1:35–50 aloud. Which of the disciples' experiences most closely resembles your own experience in deciding to follow Jesus?

When You Can't Keep the Good News to Yourself

4. Philip enthusiastically shares with Nathanael the good news that he has found the Messiah. Rather than share in the excitement, Nathanael asks whether any good thing can come out of Nazareth. The response isn't exactly what Philip hoped for! Have you ever had someone share their faith with you? Describe your response.

Have you ever shared your faith and the response wasn't what you had hoped for? How did you handle the situation?

NOTABLE

Jesus responds to Nathanael by acknowledging that he's an Israelite in whom there's nothing deceitful or false. The wording of the statement suggests that Nathanael is different from Jacob (before his name changed to Israel) in that he is honest and true.

5. Sometimes those who are the most cynical have the deepest hungers and desires that have gone unmet. Nathanael's response to Philip's news that he's found the Messiah is marked by cynicism.

What are some specific situations that you've encountered in the last three months that have tempted you to respond with cynicism?

What do you think is the best way to respond to someone with cynical views of God and Christianity?

6. Are you inviting people on a regular basis, as Philip did, to "come and see" Jesus? Why or why not?

7. What compels or hinders you from sharing your faith?

BONUS ACTIVITY

If you're into astronomy, you're probably familiar with "The Sword of Orion" from the constellation Orion. To learn more about this image, go online and Google images from the Hubble Telescope as well as this constellation. Thank God for the beauty of creation.

8. Are there some ways you've seen God work to draw people to himself that make you uncomfortable or quietly think, "I wish God *didn't* work that way"? If so, describe. Are there ways in which God works to draw people closer that you love to see? If so, describe.

Come and See

9. Are there any methods, techniques, or conversation starters that you've personally found effective for sharing your faith? If you were to create a "Five Best Practices" list for sharing your faith, what would you place on the list?

10. The Gospel of John is written so that people will not only encounter Jesus but believe in Jesus. Read John 20:30–31.

From this first lesson, what details, stories, or interactions would lead you to believe in Jesus?

Have you ever seen someone's life transformed in a beautiful way because they chose to believe in Jesus? If so describe.

Jesus is in the business of drawing people into a beautiful relationship with himself. We have the opportunity to share the good news of who Jesus is and all that he has done and, in the process, to bring people to Jesus so they grow in their faith and knowledge of him.

CLOSE IN PRAYER

Ask God to:

- Give you courage to share your faith both in words and actions.
- Provide opportunities to introduce people to Jesus as well as sensitivity to when those moments arrive.
- Make the good news truly *good* news in your life so that it bubbles out of you.

JUMPSTART

To prepare for the next group session, read John 4:1–45 and tackle the Afterhours personal studies.

BONUS ACTIVITY

Take a quick photo! If your group is meeting for the first time, before you close take a picture of yourselves and email it to info@margaretfeinberg.com. Your group could be featured soon on the home page of www.margaretfeinberg.com.

Afterhours Personal Studies

Dive deeper into John's Gospel by engaging in these five personal studies. If you only have time for one, choose Day Five, which will prepare you specifically for the next session.

DAY ONE: The Uniqueness of John's Gospel

JOHN 1:1–5

All four of the Gospels tell the stories of Jesus in a unique way. Matthew provides a detailed account of Jesus' actions and interactions. Mark's Gospel is short, sweet, and gets straight to the point about Jesus. Luke is written from the perspective of a doctor and businessman. If you want to dive into the miracles of Jesus or learn more about what Jesus thinks of financial issues, study the Gospel of Luke.

Then there's John, an artist who goes beyond the facts about Jesus to communicate the personality, the emotions, the very presence of Christ in history. John's Gospel adds color and vibe and hue to the gospel story. This beautifully written account is lined with distinctive snapshots of Jesus, his teaching, and his heart for our world.

All of the Gospels help people encounter Jesus in different ways. Let's look at the distinct ways each of the four Gospels begins.

1. Read Matthew 1:1–17. As a Jewish disciple of Jesus, Matthew begins by looking at the family tree of Jesus in order to emphasize Jesus as the legitimate King of Israel. What does Matthew's introduction reveal about his purpose for writing? Make a list of three to five words that describe Matthew's writing style (for example: *logical, detailed, in-depth*).

2. Read Mark 1:1–8. Directed toward a Roman audience, Mark uses a completely different method of reaching his audience than Matthew. What does Mark's introduction reveal about his purpose for writing? Make a list of three to five words that describe Mark's writing style.

QUOTABLE

The essence of the depth of John's picture of Jesus is its simplicity. Light, water, bread, seed sown. Jesus is revealed through the immediate, the tangible. He left out the parables of Jesus because, for John, Jesus' entire life was a parable; a parable of misunderstanding, of pain, of joy."[20]

—Michael Card

3. Read Luke 1:1–4. Unlike Matthew, Luke traces Jesus' lineage all the way to Adam. What does Luke's introduction reveal about his purpose for writing? Make a list of three to five words that describe Luke's writing style.

NOTABLE

John was written significantly later than the other three Gospels. Thus, the author of John's Gospel would have been aware of the other Gospels (especially Mark), but pointedly chose specific instances and personal interactions with Jesus to express in his Gospel.

4. Read John 1:1–5. Instead of beginning with Adam and the first human, John begins even before then. John paints a breathtakingly beautiful portrait of the reality of God incarnate in the person of Jesus Christ. What does John's introduction reveal about his purpose for writing? Make a list of three to five words that describe John's writing style.

5. Which of these four approaches to telling the story of Jesus appeals to your own personality and learning style?

BONUS ACTIVITY

Logos was a term used by ancient Greek philosophers to refer to a higher power. While these philosophers only theorized that God existed, the Gospel of John uses this term to suggest that God isn't a mere theory; God not only exists but is revealed in Jesus. Spend some time researching *logos* in *Strong's Concordance* under GK 3364.

6. Why is it important to study the stories of Jesus? How has studying the stories of Jesus within the Gospels affected your faith in the past?

Spend some time asking God to whet your appetite to know God even more! Ask God to increase your hunger to study Scripture and celebrate the discoveries you make along the way.

DAY TWO: Seeing Jesus in Images, Titles, and Roles

JOHN 1

Throughout the first chapter of John, a wide variety of images, titles, and roles are used in order to introduce readers to Jesus. Since John's Gospel is written to a diverse audience, John describes Jesus using beautiful imagery that appeals to a wide audience—Greeks, Romans, Gentiles, and Jews. Jesus came to save all of humanity, not just a particular people group.

1. Read John 1. Use the following chart to write down the images, titles, or roles John uses to describe Jesus.

SCRIPTURE	IMAGES, TITLES, OR ROLES THAT DESCRIBE JESUS
John 1:1	
John 1:4	
John 1:5, 9	
John 1:14	
John 1:15	
John 1:18	
John 1:26, 36	
John 1:34	
John 1:38	
John 1:41	
John 1:45	
John 1:49	

2. Identifying Jesus as the Word (or Logos), life, and light provide a cosmic perspective of Jesus. Jesus was not only with God in the beginning, but creation did not happen apart from Jesus. Life is found in Jesus, not just through creation, but also through the reconciliation of humanity to God through the person of Jesus.

According to this chapter, what role does Jesus play in creation?

What is the significance of Jesus being incarnate—fully divine and fully human?

How do you think your relationship with God would be different if Jesus had not been fully human?

NOTABLE

Nathanael calls Jesus "the king of Israel" in John 1:49, a term that only appears in the New Testament three times, another of which is also in John's Gospel: Jesus' triumphal entry into Jerusalem (John 12:13). The third mention is in Matthew 27:42.

3. What do the images, titles, and roles reveal about Jesus' relationship with God? (*Hint:* See John 1:14, 15, 18, 29, 34, 36.)

4. What do the images, titles, and roles reveal about Jesus' role in relationship to the people of Israel? (*Hint:* See John 1:37, 41, 45, 49.)

5. What do the images, titles, and roles allude to regarding Jesus' future death and resurrection? (*Hint:* See John 1:29, 36.)

NOTABLE

John's Gospel uses the term *king* sixteen times and almost always refers to Jesus, suggesting the importance of his royalty.

6. Of all the images, titles, and roles for Jesus mentioned in this chapter, which one is most beautiful and meaningful to you? And how is it significant for you right now?

Spend some time in prayer asking God to reveal Jesus to you in a fresh way. Ask God to open up the understanding of your mind and heart to comprehend and embrace the reality of Jesus in your life during the upcoming weeks.

DAY THREE: Creating and Cleansing

JOHN 2

After introducing us to Jesus, John highlights seven miracles called "signs" which point to Jesus as the much-anticipated Messiah. The first of these signs is a somewhat startling event. Jesus unexpectedly turns water into wine for a wedding celebration. The dramatic and prophetic act is meant to demonstrate Jesus' divine power and lead the reader to believe that Jesus is the Messiah. The Greek word for the "good" wine Jesus creates is *kalos*, which can be translated "beautiful." Thus the miracle Jesus performs is creating beautiful wine.

1. Read John 2:1–12. The passage begins with the words, "On the third day." Three days seems to be significant throughout Scripture. According to the passages in the chart on the next page, what other events happened on the third day?

SCRIPTURE	ON THE THIRD DAY . . .
Genesis 22:1–12	*Example: Abraham journeys to Mount Moriah to offer Isaac as a sacrifice. On the third day, Abraham arrives only to have an angel stop him before he can kill his son.*
Genesis 40:12–23	
Hosea 6:1–2	
John 2:19	
1 Corinthians 15:3–8	

Reflecting on these passages, what does the third day represent or symbolize to you?

Weddings in ancient culture lasted anywhere from three days to an entire week. Often the entire community—including friends and family—were involved in the celebration, placing a considerable burden on the host family. Jesus is attending a wedding in the small town of Cana in Galilee along with his disciples when his mother announces the hosts are out of wine.

Running out of wine in ancient culture meant public disgrace and shame. Jesus' brusque response to the immediate need for wine suggests he isn't overly concerned with the family's social faux pas. Rather than call his mother by her first name, he asks, "Woman, why do you involve me? My hour has not yet come." It is worth noting that throughout John's Gospel, Jesus' mother is never identified as Mary.

Mary doesn't waiver. She has no idea what her son will do, but she trusts he will do what's best. Mary tells the servants to do whatever Jesus instructs.

NOTABLE
Though debated, some scholars suggest that running out of wine at the wedding may be symbolic of the barrenness of Judaism. They also believe the six ceremonial stone jars, rather than having the perfect number of seven, point to the imperfection and inadequacy of the Jewish law. Jesus' provision of choice wine suggests that his provision is superior to the law.

Jesus instructs the servants to fill six stone ceremonial jars (totaling somewhere between 120 and 180 gallons) with water. Then he asks that some be taken to the master of the banquet who has no idea of the sequence of events that led to the tasting. Like a sommelier, the master comments on the high quality of the wine and asks why they've saved the beautiful wine for now, when it should have been served first.

2. What does this story, the first of seven signs, reveal to you about Jesus?

What within this story persuades you that Jesus is the incarnate Word of God?

After the first sign or miracle of turning water into wine, Jesus, his mother and brothers, and the disciples travel to Capernaum. With Passover approaching, Jesus makes the first of three journeys to Jerusalem to celebrate the Passover (John 2:13; 6:4; 11:55).

Traveling to Jerusalem to celebrate a feast was not uncommon. Jews made an annual pilgrimage for three different feasts: Passover, Tabernacles, and Weeks (Pentecost). Of all of the feasts, Passover was considered the most important. The feast celebrates God's deliverance of the Jewish people from slavery in Egypt. When the death angel passed over the homes, those whose doorposts had been marked with blood had their firstborn child's life spared. (For a deeper understanding of the Passover, read Exodus 12.)

Upon arrival in the temple, Jesus encounters people selling oxen, sheep, and doves as well as exchanging money. The practices were not unusual; in fact, the pilgrims needed them. Temple practices required animals for sacrifice and it was often impractical to insist people travel long distances with their animals. In addition, the required temple tax had to be paid in the local currency. While many of the travelers probably appreciated their services, Jesus has a different response.

The focus of John's Gospel isn't to create a chronological account of Jesus' life so much as it is proclaiming the life and ministry of Christ and inviting people to believe in him. While the other Gospels feature the story of Jesus overturning the tables at the close of Jesus' ministry (Matthew 21:13; Mark 11:17; Luke 19:46), John places it at the beginning.

3. Read John 2:13–25. While salespeople and moneychangers had their place in serving the travelers to Jerusalem, they should have been conducting their business near the temple rather than *in* the temple. Their disregard shows contempt and irreverence for God. Instead of *helping* people worship God, their presence inside the temple *impeded* worship. How do you think onlookers responded to Jesus' reaction in the temple?

4. How does the image of Jesus in verses 15–16 compare and contrast with popular images of Jesus in our culture?

   How does the image of Jesus in verses 15–16 compare and contrast with your own understanding and image of Jesus?

NOTABLE
The Feast of Unleavened Bread begins with the Passover meal and continues for seven days (Exodus 12:18-19). In order to prepare for the feast, Jews search their homes and remove any bits of leavened bread. This cleansing of the house is essential to preparing for the Passover. This same image of cleansing is demonstrated in Jesus' actions in the temple.

Following Jesus' passionate display of cleansing the temple, the disciples reflect on Psalm 69:9. Some of the Jews watching the scene unfold ask for a sign. Jesus says that if they destroy the temple, then in three days he will raise it up (John 2:19). Throughout John's Gospel, Jesus will say many things that are misunderstood or misinterpreted.

5. What do you think Jesus' cleansing of the temple as well as the promise to rebuild the temple symbolizes?

How do Jesus' statements set the stage for his death and resurrection?

6. What areas of your heart do you feel need to be cleansed? What do you think Jesus would drive out of your heart?

Spend some time asking God if there are any areas of your life in which you need to ask forgiveness and make a change. Ask God to cleanse you from the inside out.

DAY FOUR: Unexpected Encounters

JOHN 3

While the wedding at Cana offered a miraculous sign of Jesus' divinity and the overturning of the tables in the temple provided a prophetic sign, John's Gospel now offers us another glimpse of Jesus and his mission.

While still in Jerusalem, Jesus is visited by Nicodemus, a wealthy member of the Sanhedrin, the Jewish ruling council composed of Sadducees and Pharisees. Since John's Gospel has already revealed Jesus as the light (John 1:5), it's no small detail that Nicodemus comes to Jesus at night and engages in a conversation that changes his life forever. The only other person to approach Jesus at night is Judas Iscariot (John 13:30).

1. Read John 3. Much speculation surrounds Nicodemus' motives and character. The fact that he visits Jesus at night suggests Nicodemus is afraid of being seen by other religious leaders. What title does Nicodemus use to address Jesus? What does this reveal about Nicodemus' attitude and respect toward Jesus? (*Hint:* See John 3:2.)

2. What are Nicodemus' main concerns?

   What does Nicodemus' response to Jesus reveal about his own spiritual life? (*Hint:* See John 3:2, 4, 9.)

3. How do you navigate situations that you find yourself in where the spiritual image you want to project is at odds with what's most true about you?

John hinted at this concept of rebirth or being born from above in the first chapter when he wrote, "But as many as received Him, to them He gave the right to become children of God, even to those who believe in His name, who were born, not of blood nor of the will of the flesh nor of the will of man, but of God" (John 1:12–13 NASB).

Yet this was not the only concept that was hard for Nicodemus to grasp. The idea that God loves the whole world must have been challenging as well. Jews rarely acknowledged God loving the world, only Israel. The idea that everyone is invited to believe and become a transformed child of God, empowered by the Spirit, through being born from above probably challenged Nicodemus on several levels.

NOTABLE

Jesus' reference to Moses lifting up the snake in the desert (John 3:14-15) can be found in Numbers 21:4-9 and highlights the need for Christ's gift of salvation.

4. Why do you think the concept of being born from above is so hard for people to grasp even today? In your own words, how would you explain being born from above or born again to someone?

5. According to John 3, what happens to those who choose to believe in Jesus? (*Hint:* See vv. 16, 18, 36.)

6. Like Nicodemus, are there any areas or situations in your life where you struggle to believe God? What makes it especially difficult for you to trust God in this area of your life?

Spend some time prayerfully acknowledging any areas of your life where you struggle to believe God. Ask God to give you the faith to believe.

DAY FIVE: A Questionable Woman

JOHN 4:1–41

Jesus turned water into wine at a wedding celebration, made a scene with moneychangers in the temple, and engaged in a nighttime theological conversation with a leading rabbi. Now John describes Jesus' encounter with a morally questionable woman at high noon at a well in Samaria. This is an unlikely meeting for multiple reasons, but John uses it to paint a beautiful portrait of redemption.

Strictly devout Jews avoided Samaria at all costs—especially when traveling from Jerusalem to Galilee—by taking the longer route around the region. Yet Jesus doesn't go around Samaria on his journey; he goes straight for it! The Scripture notes that Jesus "had to go" to Samaria (John 4:4), implying a divine leading to this region that was considered detestable by the Jews. Once he arrives, Jesus engages in a conversation with a woman who is viewed as detestable even by the Samaritans.

1. Read John 4:1–26. How does Jesus' introductory statement, "Give Me a drink" (John 4:7 NASB), set the scene for the conversation that follows?

QUOTABLE

"When Jesus talks to her and begins to speak about personal things, such as her many ex-husbands, she changes the subject to something controversial: the differences in worship between her people and the Jews. The goal isn't to gain more knowledge as much as to throw the Rabbi off her trail. It's a smoke screen to change subjects once Jesus talks about her life."[21]

—Bill McCready

2. How does the woman respond when Jesus tells her she has had five husbands and the man she is living with is not her husband (John 4:17–18)?

How might you have responded if Jesus, a stranger, named your past and current sins?

3. Read John 4:27–38. What parallels do you see between the disciples' misunderstanding of food (4:31–33) and the woman's misunderstanding of water (4:15)?

How does Jesus leverage her misunderstandings to reveal more about himself and God?

NOTABLE

The Samaritans acknowledge Jesus as the "Savior of the world" (John 4:42). The only other time this expression occurs in the New Testament is 1 John 4:14. The title suggests that Jesus is the one who delivers and saves from disaster. The reference to "world" suggests that Jesus didn't just come for one people group but for all people everywhere.

4. Read John 4:39–45. Why do you think the woman's fellow villagers listened to her when she returned from the well and told them about Jesus?

5. The Samaritan woman's story is a reminder that just because you may have a tarnished history in your community doesn't mean you can't share what God has done in your life. Sometimes the story will actually have a bigger effect, not a lesser one. The Samaritan woman used her story (about Jesus knowing her as well as her failures and sins) to tell others about Christ. What is the one thing in your life for which you are most grateful for God's forgiveness and redemption?

6. Rather than hiding your past sins, your past failures—the things for which you have received God's forgiveness—there may be something you can share with others as a way of telling the story of what God has done for you. Who in your life might benefit from hearing your story?

Spend some time reflecting on the work God has done in your life. How can you be more intentional about reaching out and responding to God's presence in your life? Where are the modern-day wells in your community where you can go to engage people and share the love of Christ with them? Prayerfully consider how God may want you to engage others like the Samaritan woman.

When God Sees Through You

John 4-8

Never lose an opportunity of seeing anything that is beautiful; for beauty is God's handwriting—a wayside sacrament. Welcome it in every fair face, in every fair sky, in every fair flower, and thank God for it as a cup of blessing.
—RALPH WALDO EMERSON

The human heart is embedded with an unquenchable desire for beauty. The longing for beauty expresses itself in the details of everyday life—the use of a decorative tablecloth, a fresh bouquet of flowers, a silver button on a coat. The desire for beauty awakens something in us whether lingering to watch a canary-yellow ball of fire melt into the horizon on a summer's eve or waiting for that same heavenly object to glide into the sky during a late winter morning.

God instilled in us a desire for beauty so that we would long for God from whom all beauty emanates. Though we are created to find ourselves captivated by God, we often find ourselves distracted by the imperfections in our world and ourselves. When we look at the reflection of our own humanity, we can't help but shrink back at the frailty, the flaws, the defects, and the deficiencies. At times, we want to hide. Yet God continues pursuing us, exposing those areas so they can be restored and we can walk in the wholeness and beauty God intended all along. In the process, God performs a beautiful work in our lives.

Throughout the Gospel of John, Jesus reveals that which is hidden, those areas which hold people back from believing in him. Jesus doesn't just see people; he sees through them. The Son of God sees through their facades and efforts to make a good first impression, straight to their hearts. John describes Jesus as a light that penetrates the darkness, revealing things we may not want to be seen. Often such exposure is the first step toward believing and experiencing God's healing and redemption.

GETTING STARTED: Select One (10-15 minutes)

Experiential Activity: Hidden Pictures

What you'll need:

- Images that contain hidden pictures
- Photocopies of the images or a laptop and video projector to display the images

1. Selected a handful of images that contain hidden pictures from books like the Where's Waldo? series or a *Highlights* magazine. Google the work of Liu Bolin, a camouflage master who creates unusual artwork.
2. Distribute photocopies to participants or display the pictures on a laptop or projector and spend about 5 minutes hunting for the hidden images. (Be sure to note if there are any restrictions on duplicating the image or if it is necessary to secure permission to reproduce the image.)
3. Discuss the following questions:
   - What does it feel like to find a hidden image?
   - Once you recognize the hidden image, is it hard for you not to see it? Why or why not?

Icebreaker Question

*If you're not doing the experiential activity, choose **one** of the following questions to begin your discussion.*

- What advice would you suggest for newcomers to your area to get to know people?
- When you feel threatened, do you tend to go into fight mode, flight mode, or freeze mode, and why do you think you choose that mode of response?
- The Bible never tells us the name of the woman whom Jesus met at the well, but imagine that you had the opportunity to meet her and give her a name. What name would you give her that represents her life *before* meeting Jesus and *after* meeting Jesus?

VIDEO EIGHT: When God Sees Through You (20 minutes)

As you watch the video, use the following outline to take notes on anything that stands out to you.

I sometimes convince myself that somehow God doesn't see me. That somehow I, too, can hide in plain sight.

Jesus knows that defilement or real dirtiness doesn't come from the outside but the inside—that our worst enemy is not "those people" but ourselves.

"Give me a drink." With only four words, Jesus breaks down the barriers of gender, politics, and religion.

The Samaritan woman cannot contain the good news. She becomes the first recognized female evangelist.

Though we try to empty our bag of tricks—standing perfectly still, moving excessively fast, or diverting attention elsewhere —God sees and exposes us. The exposure is always an invitation to healing, restoration, and wholeness.

GROUP DISCUSSION QUESTIONS (30–45 minutes)

1. Consider what you learned about this beautiful portrait of redemption in the life of the Samaritan woman from the Afterhours personal studies or on the video. What caught your attention or stood out most to you?

Reaching Out to "Those People"

2. Take turns reading John 4:1–42. The passage makes it clear that Jews in Jesus' day held many prejudices about Samaritans. Who would you say are the Samaritans in our society? Identify eight to ten types of people who might be classified as social outcasts—those who are marginalized or considered misfits—or those in our society whom religious people especially might look down on.

   What characteristics do these groups share?

NOTABLE
Calling a Jewish person a Samaritan was considered a hostile insult in ancient culture.

3. Have you ever been the one who is marginalized or looked down on? How did you handle the situation?

4. How do you tend to respond to people who are different from you?

5. What makes it difficult for you to relate to or reach out to the Samaritans in your own life?

Overcoming the Force Field

One of the ways Jesus demonstrates love for the Samaritan woman is by not excusing or overlooking what she's done (John 4:16–18). Jesus doesn't just see the Samaritan woman; he sees through her actions and responses and identifies the deeper issues in her life.

6. What does it mean to have compassion on those who are struggling with sin without overlooking or approving the sin? When have you experienced such a response from others in your own spiritual journey?

QUOTABLE
"A feature of this story is the way the woman persistently attempts to avoid the issues that Jesus raises. But just as persistently Jesus brings her back to them until finally he secures the desired result."[22]
—Leon Morris

7. After encountering Jesus, the woman left her water jar at the well. Why do you think the woman left her jar?

What do you think the water jar symbolizes or represents in the life of the Samaritan woman (John 4:28)?

Exposed to God's Healing

8. Pair up with one other person. Take turns reading aloud each of the passages listed on the chart that follows. After each passage, briefly discuss what the passage reveals about God's mercy and compassion and how you see these same truths reflected in the story of Jesus and the Samaritan woman. Briefly note your responses in the space provided.

SCRIPTURE	GOD'S MERCY AND COMPASSION IN SCRIPTURE	JESUS' MERCY AND COMPASSION FOR THE SAMARITAN WOMAN
Exodus 33:19		
Deuteronomy 4:30–31		
Psalm 103:13		
Hebrews 4:15–16		

9. Read Revelation 7:16–17. What hope is promised for those who thirst and hunger?

In what ways would this passage be a source of comfort for both the Samaritan woman and the disciples?

In what ways does this passage comfort you?

10. While knowing that God sees everything can be challenging and make us wish that we could leave some things in the dark, there's also great comfort in this truth. What comfort do you find in knowing that God sees everything in your life? What are you glad that God sees and knows?

CLOSE IN PRAYER

Ask God to:

- Reveal areas in your life that need healing, restoration, and wholeness.
- Trade any ashes in your life for beauty.
- Help you find opportunities to reach out to those on the margins of your community and share his love and faithfulness.

JUMPSTART

To prepare for the next group session, read John 9 and tackle the Afterhours personal studies.

SESSION EIGHT

Afterhours Personal Studies

Dive deeper into John's Gospel by engaging in these five personal studies. If you only have time for one, choose Day Five, which will prepare you specifically for the next session.

DAY ONE: Divine Healings and Declarations

JOHN 4:46–5:45

After spending time in Samaria, Jesus returns to Cana where he performed the miracle of making water into wine and performs another miracle (John 4:54). This particular miracle is unusual in that it's one of the long-distance miracles that Jesus performed (see Matthew 8:5–13; Luke 7:1–19). The act highlights Jesus' divinity as well as the royal official's faith.

1. Read John 4:46–54. What do you find surprising in the royal official's response to Jesus (vv. 48–49)?

Would you have responded to Jesus in the same way after hearing his comment? Why or why not?

After returning to Cana, Jesus travels back to Jerusalem for an unspecified feast. Walking by the pool at Bethesda, Jesus has compassion on a specific man who had been sick for 38 years. In a strikingly beautiful moment, Jesus heals him.

NOTABLE

Some scholars believe the "sheep gate" (Nehemiah 3:1, 32; 12:39) was a small opening in the temple wall where the sheep entered and were washed before being taken into the sanctuary for sacrifice. The nearby pool became a waiting area for the sick and disabled who hoped for a miraculous healing.

2. Read John 5:1–17. Why do you think the response to the healing of the official's son is so much different than the response to the healing of the sick man at the pool of Bethesda?

What three things does Jesus do and say that make the Jews so angry? (*Hint:* See John 5:9, 16–18.)

3. The story focuses more on the controversy that follows the healing rather than the healing itself. Why is this significant?

Do you tend to become more or less involved in religious communities that are concerned with controversy? Explain.

Opposition toward Jesus grows to the point the Jews want to kill him. Jesus offers a response in the form of a monologue. The lack of follow-up questions from listeners may suggest that Jesus silenced their concerns (though opposition only increases in upcoming chapters) or may suggest a literary device used in John's Gospel to sum up Jesus' thoughts on a situation.

4. Read John 5:18–47. What are the primary claims Jesus makes within this passage?

SCRIPTURE	JESUS' CLAIM	WHY THIS CLAIM WOULD ANGER THE JEWISH RELIGIOUS LEADERS
John 5:18	*Example: God as his Father; making himself equal with God*	*Example: The Jews thought it was wrong to claim to be equal with God.*
John 5:24		
John 5:27, 30		
John 5:46–47		

5. In this monologue, Jesus names four witnesses that affirm his identity as the Messiah. Who/what are they? (*Hint:* See John 5:33, 36, 37, 39.)

Where do you turn when you need your faith strengthened?

6. The first five chapters of John offer beautiful stories of Jesus' miracles and teachings. Through Jesus, God's life-giving activity is unleashed among the people. Jesus' teachings confirm what people are seeing and experiencing through the miracles. Which of the miracles Jesus performed is most meaningful to you in your own faith journey right now?

Spend some time reflecting on the claims Jesus makes in John 5 about who he really is. Prayerfully ask God to make these claims more real in your own life. Over the upcoming week, keep an eye out for people and situations that witness that Jesus is the Messiah.

DAY TWO: Unforgettable Miracles Surrounding the Passover

JOHN 6

Jesus displays the beauty and wonder of his divinity through a wide array of miracles and rich teachings in the first five chapters of John's Gospel. In the sixth chapter, Passover is mentioned for a second time. This is significant to the events that are about to unfold. During the Passover, the Jewish people studied the Scriptures that described the Israelites' escape from Egypt. They were reading about God's miraculous provision and protection—the narrow escape through the Red Sea and the feeding of the Israelites in the desert—when Jesus performs two unforgettable miracles.

Jesus is attracting sizeable crowds. Some want to hear his teachings, but many just want to see the healings and miracles. Looking out on the thousands of followers, many of whom have traveled long distances, Jesus performs a miracle that is reminiscent of God feeding the Israelites in the desert.

1. Read John 6:1–14. Jesus already knows he is going to perform a miracle. Jesus asks Philip where to buy bread, but Philip is too distracted by the cost of feeding so many people. Meanwhile, Andrew finds the only source of bread and fish available, but then questions how the food could ever be enough. Philip becomes overwhelmed by the size of the issue; Andrew becomes overwhelmed by the

insufficiency of a possible solution. Neither recognizes Jesus' ability to perform the miraculous. When you are faced with a difficult challenge, does your response tend to be more like Philip's or Andrew's? Why?

NOTABLE

John 6:9 notes that the boy's five loaves were made of barley, a food which was common among the poor since it had a less desirable flavor. Wealthy people preferred wheat bread, which cost at least twice as much. This suggests that it was a poor boy that gave his food to Jesus.

2. Read John 6:14–25. Jesus identifies himself to the disciples as "It is I" when approaching them on the water (John 6:20). Throughout the Gospel of John, Jesus proclaims multiple "I AM" statements. The Greek *ego eimi* is emphatic—literally translating "I, I am." The words are reminiscent of God revealing himself as "I AM" in Exodus 3:14. If Jesus' feeding of the multitude is reminiscent of God providing for the Israelites in the desert (Exodus 16), then what is Jesus' walking on the water reminiscent of in the history of the Israelites? (*Hint:* See Exodus 13–15.)

Jesus knows the response of the people to the miracle will be to take him by force and make him king. Jesus withdraws to the mountains near Galilee. The disciples travel ahead by boat to Capernaum.

The miracles of feeding the five thousand and walking on water demonstrate that Jesus is the Messiah and fulfilling the role of God. Jesus is feeding, providing, protecting, guarding, rescuing, leading, and teaching. Though the people face challenges on every front—from lack of food to severe weather—Jesus overcomes every one of them. The miracles Jesus performs are reminiscent of God's care for the Israelites surrounding the events of Passover.

3. Read John 6:26–40. What does Jesus communicate about the true bread of God in the following verses?

SCRIPTURE	TRUE BREAD OF GOD
John 6:32	*Example: The bread that was provided in the desert didn't come from Moses, but from God.*
John 6:33	
John 6:34	

4. Read John 6:41–65. What portion of this teaching do you think was the hardest for the Jews to believe? Why?

What portion of this teaching is the hardest for you to believe?

BONUS ACTIVITY

The Israelites were known as God's chosen people in the Old Testament. Jesus now refers to his disciples, the community of believers, as those he has chosen (John 6:70). Read Numbers 11. What parallels do you see between the miracle of Jesus providing for the multitudes and God providing for the Israelites?

5. Read John 6:66–71. How does the response of many of the disciples (v. 66) compare with Peter's response (vv. 68–69)?

What does this passage reveal about what it means to believe in Jesus?

6. In what areas of your own spiritual life do you find yourself struggling with unbelief?

Spend some time prayerfully reflecting on John 6 and the teachings of Jesus. Ask God to reveal any areas of unbelief in your life. Ask him for the wisdom, grace, and courage to believe. Ask him to give you a spiritual appetite for the food which endures.

DAY THREE: When Opposition Mounts

JOHN 7

Opposition and controversy surround Jesus on every side. Even his own family members are questioning his identity. Though they've seen the miracles, they refuse to believe. John's Gospel is written so that people might believe in Jesus, but this chapter reveals that many people choose to oppose Jesus instead.

1. Read John 7:1–53. What criticism, hostility, or opposition does Jesus face in each of the following passages? On a scale of 1 to 10 (1 being low, 10 being high), how would you rate the level of criticism, hostility, or opposition?

SCRIPTURE	CRITICISM, HOSTILITY, OR OPPOSITION FACED	LEVEL OF OPPOSITION
John 7:1	*Example: Jews are trying to kill Jesus.*	*Example: 10*
John 7:5		
John 7:7		
John 7:12		
John 7:15		

(cont.)

SCRIPTURE	CRITICISM, HOSTILITY, OR OPPOSITION FACED	LEVEL OF OPPOSITION
John 7:20		
John 7:27		
John 7:30		
John 7:32		
John 7:42		
John 7:43		

Among the examples of criticism, hostility, and opposition you listed on the chart, which two or three do you think are most often expressed about Jesus today?

2. How does Jesus respond to the criticism, hostility, and opposition he faces?

What insights do you gain from Jesus' example about how to face criticism, hostility, or opposition in your own life?

NOTABLE

Jesus is questioned on where he went to school (John 7:15), where he is from (John 7:27), and where he is going (John 7:35). The irony is, the answer to all three questions is the same: heaven.

Jews in Jesus' day traveled to Jerusalem for three annual feasts—the Feast of Passover (mentioned three times in John's Gospel), the Feast of Pentecost which is seven weeks after the Passover and celebrates the harvest of grain, and the Feast of Tabernacles which celebrates the fall harvest. Jesus often uses images from these festivals in his teachings. In the seventh chapter of John, Jesus draws on rich imagery from the Feast of Tabernacles.

The Feast of Tabernacles is also referred to as the Feast of Booths or Ingathering because, in order to protect the harvest, farmers had to build shelters in the fields. The image of a temporary shelter is reminiscent of the temporary shelters the Israelites built in the desert to survive. Thus, the Feast of Tabernacles, or Sukkot, which is still celebrated today, is more than a fall harvest; the holy days are used to study and reflect on the desert wanderings of the Israelites.

Sacrifices were offered throughout the seven-day Festival of the Tabernacles celebration. Since fall is a dry season, requests were also made for rain, including a water ceremony in which a priest filled a golden pitcher with water as a choir quoted Isaiah 12:3. The water was then carried back up to the "Water Gate" at the temple with crowds singing Psalms 113–118. Then the water was poured out on the altar as an offering. On the final day of the Feast of Tabernacles, the water ceremony was repeated seven times.

3. Reflecting on the context of this scene, why are Jesus' statements in John 7:37–39 significant?

4. How do you respond to opposition and criticism in your life?

5. On the continuum below, how would you rate your own response to opposition and criticism?

A Healthy Response   Unhealthy Response

6. What steps can you take to developing or maintaining a healthy response to criticism and opposition?

Ask God to give you wisdom and grace to face opposition and criticism. Then spend some time asking God to unleash rivers of living water in your life. Ask God to both increase and quench your spiritual thirst.

DAY FOUR: A Spiritual Ambush

JOHN 8

Jesus travels to the Mount of Olives. As if Jesus isn't surrounded by enough controversy, he's now faced with a spiritual ambush. The religious leaders present Jesus with a woman caught in adultery, but her story is only incidental to the main show—forcing Jesus to make a judgment on a hot-button issue.

1. Read John 8:1–11. How would you describe the demeanor or attitude of the various people in the story?

The woman caught in adultery

The religious leaders

The onlookers

Jesus

BONUS ACTIVITY

For Old Testament background of the charges against the adulterous woman, read Leviticus 20:10 and Deuteronomy 22:22.

2. Some scholars suggest Jesus may have written Exodus 23:1 and Jeremiah 17:13 in the dust. Look up each passage. Why do you think scholars suggest these passages as the ones Jesus wrote in the dust?

After the woman accused of adultery goes free, Jesus makes some startling claims. Jesus declares himself the light of the world—a metaphor first introduced in John 1:4–5—and then goes on to make even more provocative claims.

3. Read John 8:12–29. How do the Pharisees respond to Jesus' claim to be the light of the world (v. 13)?

How does Jesus answer the Pharisees (vv. 14–18)?

Why do you think Jesus' claim is so hard for the Pharisees to accept?

NOTABLE

Just as Jesus' claim to be the living water tied into the Feast of Tabernacles, Jesus' claim to be the light of the world also tied into the celebration. Each night during the festival, large oil candles were lit. They traditionally unraveled the old garments of the priests and used the material as wicks. Many believe that Jesus' declaration of being the light of the world was in the context of this familiar scene.

4. What controversial claim does Jesus make in each of the following verses?

SCRIPTURE	CONTROVERSIAL CLAIM
John 8:19	
John 8:24	
John 8:32	
John 8:42	
John 8:44	
John 8:58	

With each statement, tensions escalate between the religious leaders and Jesus. Every statement is met with misunderstanding and disbelief. The religious leaders accuse Jesus of being a Samaritan as well as being possessed by a demon. By claiming Jesus is a Samaritan, the religious leaders are severing him from any connection with Judaism and the children of Abraham. By claiming he has a demon, the religious leaders are trying to connect Jesus with the devil instead of God.

Despite the misunderstandings, attacks, and disbelief, Jesus continues to proclaim the good news and invite belief; whoever obeys his word, he says, will be spared and never taste death (John 8:51). This, too, is misunderstood and dismissed by the religious leaders (vv. 52–53).

The irony of this chapter is that it began with Jesus defending a woman from being stoned. Fifty-nine verses later the religious leaders are picking up rocks to stone Jesus.

5. Briefly review your responses to question 1. Throughout the course of your spiritual journey, in what ways, if any, have you responded to Jesus as those people did?

The woman caught in adultery

The religious leaders

The onlookers

Spend time in prayer asking God for what you need right now. Your requests may include humility, grace, peace, love, or greater compassion for others. Express your gratitude to God for the ways he has extended compassion to you.

DAY FIVE: Open the Eyes of Our Hearts

JOHN 9

The healing of the blind man in John's Gospel is the sixth of John's seven signs. Here's a quick summary of all seven signs:

1. Changing water into wine (John 2:1–11).
2. Cleansing the temple (John 2:13–22).
3. Healing the nobleman's son (John 4:46–54).
4. Healing the lame man (John 5:1–15).
5. Feeding the multitude (John 6:1–15).
6. Healing the blind man (John 9:1–12).
7. Raising Lazarus from the dead (John 11). (We'll study this sign in session nine.)

While healing the blind man is the sixth sign, it is only the third healing recorded in John's Gospel.

One can only imagine what the man's response was to all the beauty he encountered once his eyes were opened. Colors unimaginable. Hues unexpected. Inconceivable scenes surrounded him in every direction.

1. Read John 9:1–12. Restoring sight to the blind was known as a messianic sign in the Old Testament. Reflecting on the following passages, how does Jesus' healing recorded here in John reveal himself as the long awaited and promised Messiah?

   Isaiah 29:18

   Isaiah 35:5

   Isaiah 42:7

2. God can open physical eyes and God can open spiritual eyes, which are sometimes called the eyes of the heart. What would you like God to reveal to you or help you see more clearly in your life?

Jewish rabbis maintained a belief that suffering and sin were connected. Thus, the Jewish culture embraced the belief that any suffering was somehow linked to sin, whether or not it could be identified. While Jesus acknowledges that suffering can be a result of sin, it is not always the case and this truth will be demonstrated in the life of the blind man.

The healing of the blind man draws on two images that are used repeatedly in John's Gospel: water and light. Jesus reveals himself as the "living water" (John 7:38) and the "light of the world" (John 9:5).

Water references saturate the pages of John's Gospel:

- The book begins with John the Baptist baptizing people in the Jordan River (John 1:26).
- Jesus' first miracle is turning water into wine (John 2:6–9).
- Jesus tells Nicodemus of the importance of being born of water and spirit (John 3:5).
- Jesus meets the Samaritan woman at a well (John 4).
- Jesus displays his power by walking on water in the middle of a storm (John 6:16–19).
- When Jesus reveals himself as the "living water" he does so with the backdrop of the water ceremony as part of the Feast of Tabernacles (John 7:38).

Now Jesus places a blend of saliva and dirt on a blind man's eyes and sends him to wash in the Pool of Siloam, the very source of the water for the water-pouring ceremony at the Feast of Tabernacles.

References to light illuminate John's Gospel:

- Jesus is referred to as the light in the cosmic poem that opens the book (John 1:4–5, 9).
- Jesus reveals to Nicodemus that those who live by the truth enter the light (John 3:21).
- With the rich backdrop of the lighting ceremonies of the Feast of Tabernacles, Jesus reveals himself as the light of the world (John 8:12).
- Before opening the eyes of the blind man, Jesus announces that he's the light of the world (John 9:5).

The imagery of both water and light come together in the healing of the blind man, whose physical blindness is contrasted against the spiritual blindness of the religious leaders.

3. In what ways is the beautiful healing of the blind man a fulfillment of Jesus' claim to be the light of the world?

4. Read John 9:13–41. Why do you think the healing of the blind man creates such a controversy?

How do you think the blind man felt as he experienced healing?

How do you think the blind man felt when he heard the reaction from the following people?

Neighbors

Religious leaders

His own parents

Which do you think was the most hurtful? Why?

5. The Pharisees excommunicate the blind man, but Jesus seeks him out—another example of how Jesus takes the initiative to pursue those he loves. We saw this in session seven when Jesus sought out his disciples, calling them to follow him (page 156). In what ways do you think Jesus may be pursuing you right now—to bring something hidden to light, to give your thirsty soul a drink of cold water, or to help you in some other way?

Spend time prayerfully asking God to reveal himself as the light of your life and to unleash his light in the deepest areas of your being. Ask God to create opportunities for you to shine his light to the world.

Recognizing the Blind Spots

John 9–11

In a gracious gratitude men are affected with the attribute of God's goodness and free grace not only as they are concerned in it, or as it affects their interest, but as part of the glory and beauty of God's nature. That wonderful and unparalleled grace of God, which is manifested in the work of redemption, and shines forth in the face of Jesus Christ, is infinitely glorious in itself and appears so to the angels; it is a great part of the moral perfection and beauty of God's nature.[23]

—JONATHAN EDWARDS

Though the beauty of God beckons us, we can close our eyes to God's beauty—not only in creation but in our own lives. We can become blind to the moments when God wants to apprehend us with goodness, call us to holiness, and ignite our hearts with love.

All of us have blurred vision in one area or another. We also have blind spots—both physically and spiritually. Yet Jesus is the one who opens our eyes so that we can see clearly and recognize the beautiful work he's doing in our lives. May we live with eyes wide open to recognize the beauty of God in all its expressions.

GETTING STARTED: Select One (10-15 minutes)

Experiential Activity: When Love Comes to Town

What you'll need:

- Three to five simple and tasty foods for people to eat
- A few blindfolds—bandanas or scarves work well

1. Purchase three to five different yummy foods that require little to no preparation to eat (for example, apples, honeydew, cupcakes, crackers, and cheese).
2. Ask participants to close their eyes and tie on a blindfold.
3. Distribute food samples one at a time. (Check to see if anyone has food allergies before serving samples.)
4. Invite participants to taste the food and to identify it with as much precision as possible. For example, if they're eating a bite of apple, can they identify the type of apple—Honeycrisp, Granny Smith, or Fuji? If they are eating a cupcake, can they identify the flavor?
5. Spend some time enjoying the leftover snacks and discuss these questions:
   - What role does sight play in enjoying food?
   - What would you miss the most if you were unable to see?
   - What would you miss the least?

Icebreaker Question

*If you're not doing the experiential activity, choose **one** of the following sets of questions to begin your discussion.*

- Do you or any of your friends have an issue with your vision that inhibits your everyday life? What do you think are the biggest challenges of vision impairment? Are there any upsides to not being able to see as well?
- If you had to lose one of your senses (taste, touch, smell, hearing, or sight), which would you live without? Why did you choose it?
- Share a childhood memory in which you were confronted or surrounded by darkness. What did you feel and experience at that moment? How did the experience shape you?

VIDEO NINE: Recognizing the Blind Spots (17 minutes)

As you watch the video, use the following outline to take notes on anything that stands out to you.

What's wrong with my driving?

We all see things differently. We notice different details. And we all have blind spots—both physically and spiritually.

Instead of responding with celebration and joy to this beautiful moment, they begin interrogating the blind man.

The whole story raises the question of how often God wants to expose a blind spot in my life, and I respond like the religious leaders.

Something about being confronted by the miraculous, the transformative power of God, exposes the blind spots in our lives.

Sometimes we forget that even if we score perfectly on Bible tests, it doesn't mean our vision is 20/20.

GROUP DISCUSSION QUESTIONS (30–45 minutes)

1. Consider what you learned about this beautiful portrait of healing in the life of the blind man from the Afterhours personal studies or on the video. What caught your attention or stood out most to you?

Blind from Birth

2. Read John 9:1–12. Jesus said, "I am the light of the world." How have you experienced Jesus as a light in your own life? In other words, how has Christ's life and teaching helped you to see things —spiritual truth, personal failures, goodness—you might otherwise have missed?

How has your life been transformed by this beautiful light?

NOTABLE

Jesus heals a deaf and mute man in Mark 7 by applying saliva to the man's tongue and again in Mark 8 when he touches a blind man's eyes with saliva. Saliva was believed to have medicinal healing ability in the ancient world. Some even believed it had magical powers, which led to its use for healing being forbidden in the Jewish community.

3. After rubbing mud on the man's eyes, Jesus tells the man born blind to go and wash in the pool of Siloam. Why do you think Jesus makes such a specific yet odd demand?

4. Why do you think Jesus sometimes instantaneously heals people but at other times requires that the person make an additional effort? (See Mark 3:1–6; John 5:1–15.)

How have you experienced spiritual growth and healing in your own life? Has it been instantaneous, a step-by-step process, or perhaps a mix? Share examples, if possible, to illustrate your response.

The Controversy Brews

5. The healing of the blind man creates quite a controversy. What is the response of each of the following individuals or groups of people to the healing?

The neighbors (John 9:8–10)

The Pharisees (John 9:15–17)

The Jews (John 9:18)

The parents (John 9:20–23)

6. Despite the healing of the blind man, many still refuse to believe that Jesus is the Messiah. Are there spiritual truths you resist—things you know are true but struggle to receive or act on? What keeps you from accepting some spiritual truths?

NOTABLE

Blind Spot (noun): 1. a small area on the retina that is insensitive to light due to the interruption, where the optic nerve joins the retina, of the normal pattern of light-sensitive rods and cones. 2. An area or subject about which one is uninformed, prejudiced, or unappreciative.[24]

7. The religious leaders are so caught up in rules and regulations that they miss the bigger picture and the miraculous evidence of God's grace among them. Do you think this dynamic—focusing on rules to the point of missing grace—is a problem in the Christian community today? Why or why not?

   In what ways, if any, have you experienced this dynamic—either as the person caught up in focusing on the rules or as the recipient of graceless scrutiny from others?

8. Read John 9:35–41. Why do you think Jesus seeks out the man a second time? What does this reveal about the character of Jesus?

   Reflecting on the Afterhours study (session eight, Day Five, pages 195–199), how is this consistent with the message of John's Gospel?

Only Jesus Sees Clearly

9. How would you describe what it means to have a blind spot? If you can think of any, illustrate your response with an example from your own experience or from that of someone you know (without revealing the person's name).

If you had a blind spot about something in your life, how would you want someone to tell you about it? What could this person say or do to help you be more receptive to feedback that might be hard for you to hear?

QUOTABLE

"Christ is the genuine light. He is the light that brings real illumination to men. There is nothing unreal or shadowy about the light which is Christ."[25]

—Leon Morris

10. Jesus healed the man born blind to demonstrate the glory of God. What areas of your life—those marked by illness, weakness, failure, or inability—might God use to demonstrate his glory and beauty in your life?

Like the blind man in John's Gospel, we all have areas of our lives that we don't see clearly. Our vision is distorted and blurred and we need Jesus to open our eyes and restore our vision so we can clearly see the beautiful work that God wants to do not only in our lives but also in the lives of those around us.

CLOSE IN PRAYER

Ask God to:

- Reveal any blind spots.
- Give you his vision by helping you to see yourself and others through his eyes.
- Help you to see people or situations where you might share his love, beauty, and goodness.

JUMPSTART

To prepare for the next group session, read John 12:1–11 and tackle the Afterhours personal studies.

Afterhours Personal Studies

Dive deeper into John's Gospel by engaging in these five personal studies. If you only have time for one, choose Day Five, which will prepare you specifically for the next session.

DAY ONE: The Beautiful Shepherd

JOHN 10:1–21

Following the healing of the blind man, the Pharisees find themselves struggling to swallow Jesus' teaching. Jesus couldn't possibly be saying they're blind, could he?

Jesus affirms that because they refuse to acknowledge their blindness, because they refuse the light and the message of Jesus, they remain in the darkness of their sin. Jesus uses shepherding imagery in order to expose the hardness of their hearts and reveal himself again as the Messiah. In the process, he exposes the beautiful heart of God for each of us.

The Greek word *kalos*, which translates "good" as in "good shepherd," can also be translated as "excellent" or "beautiful." In describing himself as the good shepherd, Jesus reveals himself as the "beautiful shepherd." The beauty is displayed both in his heart and passion for the sheep as well as in his willingness to sacrifice his own life for the sheep.

1. Read John 10:1–21. Jesus' teaching describes three different types of groups caring for sheep: thieves, hirelings, true shepherds. According to this passage, how would you describe the characteristics of each group?

   Thieves

Hirelings

True shepherds

The imagery of thieves and hirelings (as opposed to true shepherds) is an indictment against the leaders of Israel who do not really love God and God's people. The imagery is used throughout the Old Testament in passages such as Psalm 23, Psalm 95, and Isaiah 40:11.

2. Read Ezekiel 34. What parallels do you see between the prophet's words to the religious leaders of Israel and Jesus' words to the religious leaders of Israel? Reflecting on the descriptions in this passage, in what ways have you felt led by the following?

Thieves

Hirelings

Good shepherds

BONUS ACTIVITY

To better understand sheep and shepherds as well as to expose some of the modern myths about sheep (i.e., the idea that they are dumb), consider reading my book *Scouting the Divine: My Search for God in Wine, Wool, and Wild Honey.*

3. What do Ezekiel 34 and John 10:1–21 reveal about God's love for you?

4. What do you believe Jesus means when he says that his sheep listen to the shepherd's voice (John 10:4)?

How do you hear and recognize God's voice in your own life?

Jesus' teaching is again met with division and a refusal to believe. Those listening accuse Jesus of having a demon and being out of his right mind just as they did in John 8:48–52. Other listeners are still debating whether Jesus really healed the blind man in John 9:16, 32–33.

NOTABLE

Before becoming a king, David was a shepherd. He is known for risking his own life for his flock in 1 Samuel 17:34–37.

5. In light of Jesus' teaching on beautiful and good shepherding, what do the religious leaders' responses reveal about their relationship to the Beautiful and Good Shepherd?

What does Jesus' teaching reveal about how they have cared for the flock, the people of God?

6. In what ways do you need Jesus to be your good shepherd right now?

Spend some time in prayer, inviting Christ to be the Good and Beautiful Shepherd who guides and protects you. You may want to use Psalm 23 as the basis for your prayer and to express gratitude for the ways God leads, guides, restores, and anoints as he shepherds you.

DAY TWO: Within God's Grasp

JOHN 10:22–42

The eight-day Feast of Dedication, also known as Hanukkah or the Feast of Lights, finds its origins in a historic event. In 167 BC, Antiochus Epiphanes captured Jerusalem and committed all kinds of atrocious acts, including erecting an altar to Zeus and offering sacrifices to Zeus in the Jewish temple. The sacrilegious acts incited guerilla warfare and, three years later, under the leadership of Judas (the Maccabee), Jerusalem was freed.

Legend has it that when the Jewish priests reentered the temple for the first time, they found a portion of holy oil sufficient to fuel a menorah (a candelabrum with nine branches) for a single day. Instead, it burned for eight days. This is the miracle celebrated today as Hanukkah, a word derived from the Hebrew verb meaning "to dedicate." During the Festival of Dedication, Jewish families use brightly lit candles and lamps throughout their homes as part of their holiday celebration.

1. Read John 10:22–42. Throughout John's Gospel, feasts and festivals are commonly used as a backdrop to the teachings of Jesus. Why might John mention the Feast of Dedication to set the stage for this particular interaction between Jesus and the religious leaders?

2. Up until this moment in John's Gospel, Jesus has only revealed himself directly as the Messiah to the Samaritan woman (John 4:26), yet he's demonstrated the fact through signs, miracles, and teachings. Why do you think the Jews are still asking Jesus to tell them plainly if he's the Messiah?

NOTABLE

John 10:22 notes a somewhat odd detail, namely, that it was winter. While some scholars argue that this detail explained why Jesus was in the sheltered area of the portico of Solomon, some suggest the wintry mention is representative of the cold attitude toward Jesus and the icy receptivity of his listeners.

3. Reflecting on the previous sessions and the Afterhours studies thus far, do you think Jesus has made it clear enough to the people that he is the Messiah? Why or why not?

4. Do you feel any frustration toward the people's unbelief? Why or why not? How do you think your feelings compare to what Jesus felt?

5. Read Leviticus 24:14. Do you think the Jews' response to Jesus in John 10:31 is appropriate based on this passage? How does Jesus answer the Jews? (*Hint:* See Psalm 82:6).

6. What comfort do you find in Jesus' promise that no one shall snatch from his hand those he gives eternal life (John 10:28)?

Spend time prayerfully reflecting on the promise that no one can snatch you out of Jesus' hand. Take a few moments to thank God for the faithfulness, love, and goodness that he's shown you.

DAY THREE: The Resurrection Power of Jesus

JOHN 11

With opposition mounting against Jesus, he withdraws to the Jordan where John the Baptist was first baptizing. As many people come to him there and believe his message, Jesus receives word from one of his supporters and followers, Mary, that her brother Lazarus is extremely ill. Rather than drop what he's doing, Jesus offers a surprising response that is reminiscent of his words about the man born blind. The sickness won't lead to death but to God's glory.

1. Read John 11:1–16. How do you resolve the conflict between Jesus' love and care for Lazarus and his deliberate choice to delay responding to Lazarus' illness?

When Jesus tells the disciples that Lazarus has fallen asleep, the disciples misinterpret Jesus and take his statement literally. Similar misinterpretations happened with the woman at the well (liquid water versus living water) and Nicodemus (physical birth versus spiritual birth). Jesus plainly tells the disciples that Lazarus is dead.

2. Read John 11:17–37. Each time Jesus is misunderstood in John's Gospel, it creates an opportunity for Jesus to reveal more about God, himself, and what he's about to do. How does Martha misunderstand what Jesus is saying (John 11:23–27)?

NOTABLE
The name Lazarus means "whom God helps."

3. How does Jesus respond to Mary, Martha, and the others who are mourning (John 11:33–35)?

Does anything surprise you or comfort you about Jesus' response?

4. Read John 11:38–46. What does this beautiful miracle reveal about Jesus' identity and mission?

5. Read John 11:47–54. What are the two different responses—the chief priests and Pharisees versus Caiaphas—toward Jesus in this passage?

What do these responses reveal about God's work in the listeners' lives?

6. In what area of your life do you most need to experience the resurrecting power of Jesus?

Spend some time asking God to reveal his resurrection power to you. Ask God to do the impossible in a specific area of your life.

DAY FOUR: The Great "I Am" Statements

Throughout John's Gospel, Jesus makes a series of "I am" sayings. The use of the "I am" is reminiscent of the name God used to reveal himself to Moses during his encounter at the burning bush in Exodus 3.

Just as the seven signs in John's Gospel reveal Jesus as the Messiah, seven "I am" statements reveal Jesus' identity, not only as the way to God but also as God. Each "I am" statement reflects a motif from Judaism that challenges listeners to recognize who Jesus is and believe in him.

1. Look up each of the following passages and record the "I am" statements in the space below:

SCRIPTURE	"I AM" STATEMENT
John 6:35	
John 8:12	
John 10:7	
John 10:11	
John 11:25	
John 14:6	

2. Jesus claims to be the bread of life (John 6:35), the spiritual food we need. Read Exodus 16:13–18. How does God reveal himself as the bread of life in this passage?

What similarities and differences do you recognize between the two kinds of spiritual sustenance—manna and Christ?

What spiritual nourishment are you most hungry for right now?

3. Jesus claims to be the light of the world (John 8:12). Read Genesis 1:3; Psalm 27:1; and Psalm 36:9. How does God reveal himself as the light of the world in these passages?

What areas of your life do you most need the light of God to shine in?

QUOTABLE

"The Father is the invisible of the Son, but the Son is the visible of the Father."[26]

—St. Irenaeus

4. Jesus reveals himself as the gate of the sheep pen and the good shepherd (John 10:7, 11). Read Psalm 23 and Ezekiel 34. How does God reveal himself as the keeper of the sheep in these passages?

How is God revealing himself as the good shepherd in your life right now?

5. Jesus describes himself as the resurrection, the way, the truth, and the life (John 11:25; 14:6). Read Deuteronomy 32:39; Psalm 86:11; and Proverbs 15:24. How does God reveal himself in similar terms in these passages?

How have you experienced God as the resurrection, the way, the truth, and the life? Are there any areas in which you have yet to experience him in these ways?

6. Jesus describes God as the vine keeper (John 15:1). Read Psalm 80:8–19 and Jeremiah 2:21–22. How does God reveal himself as the vintner or vine keeper in these passages?

Which of the metaphors or images from this personal study are most meaningful to you in your personal walk with God right now? Why?

Spend some time asking God to reveal himself more deeply and personally to you in each of these beautiful ways.

DAY FIVE: A Beautiful Act of Worship

JOHN 12:1-11

While hosting Jesus, the disciples, and various guests, Mary does something extraordinary. Mary's beautiful act probably silences the room as people watch in a strange mix of awe, wonder, and contempt.

1. Read John 12:1–11. If you were watching Mary, what might you have found most disturbing about her actions?

What would you have found to be most beautiful about her actions?

NOTABLE

The Greek word for "poured" also means "anoint." The anointing of a king by pouring oil on his head at coronation was observed not only in Israel but in other countries (Judges 9:8, 15; 1 Samuel 9:16).

2. Read John 1:27 and John 13:5. Attending to someone's feet was the work of servants. What does Mary's action reveal about her attitude toward and relationship with Christ?

3. While it's impossible to know what compelled Mary to pour out a pint of pure nard, Jesus gives the worshipful expression a theological meaning, saying the oil was poured out for his burial. (One of the first steps in preparing a body for burial was cleansing it with water and then anointing it with oil.) Why do you think Jesus describes Mary's anointing as an act of preparation for his own death?

NOTABLE

Jesus responds to Judas by referring to Deuteronomy 15:11. Though the poor are always present and though serving them is essential, this is an offering given at a particular time for a particular purpose. Jesus defends the woman and her offering, memorializing it forever.

4. Smell is incredibly powerful. Particular scents can bring back memories long past and even reignite emotions that accompanied the memories. When the fragrance of Mary's perfume fills the house, what memories do you think it may have brought to mind for the people in the room?

Mary (Luke 10:38–42)

Martha (John 11:20–25)

Lazarus (John 11:43–44)

5. What does Jesus' response reveal about his attitude toward Mary's beautiful gift?

6. When have you found yourself wondering if God is really pleased and delighted in your own gifts and offerings? What encouragement do you find in this passage that God is pleased with you and your gift?

Spend time simply worshiping God. Thank God for who he is and all that he has done in your life. Express your gratitude and adoration.

When Worship Costs More Than Expected

John 12–17

From Exodus to Revelation, worship in the Bible is clothed in gold, silver, precious stones, embroidery, robes of gorgeous fabric, bells, and candles. . . . God ordered beauty, even extravagant beauty in worship, even while His people were still wandering in the desert and living in tents.[27]
—ANTHONY CONIARIS

God desires that our relationship with him isn't lived out of a sense of duty as much as out of a sense of devotion. In other words, God longs for us to long for him. In the beauty of his presence, we can't help but find our affections set on God, our hearts captivated by his love. Caught up in the delight of God, powerful feelings of gratitude swell within us and our natural response is worship—words of thanks that roll off the tongue, songs of adoration that spring from the heart, or some other form of praise. When we give back to God, the one who has gifted us with all good things, we reflect his beauty.

When we give a meaningful gift, we often receive the affirming response we anticipated or hoped, but that's not always the case. This is particularly true of a woman who gave a very expensive and beautiful gift to Jesus.

GETTING STARTED: Select One (10–15 minutes)

Experiential Activity: Imagining the Flavors of Eden

What you'll need:

- A small bottle of nard, also known as spikenard. You'll find it online by simply Googling the spice, which is commonly bottled as an oil; spikenard may also be found at some local Christian bookstores or retailers that specialize in oils and scented products.

1. Pass around the bottle and invite participants to smell the oil.
2. Discuss the following questions:
   - What one word would you use to describe the scent?
   - Do you find anything about the scent surprising?
   - What do you think it would be like to have an entire bottle poured over your feet?
   - How long do you think the scent might remain on you and everything it touches?

Icebreaker Question

*If you're not doing the experiential activity, choose **one** of the following sets of questions to begin your discussion.*

- Describe the most meaningful gift you've ever been given. How did the gift make you feel?
- What's the single most meaningful gift you've ever given someone else? How did giving the gift make you feel?
- In what ways does giving gifts reflect God's heart for us?
- What is your all-time favorite scent? What memories does it bring to mind?

VIDEO TEN: When Worship Costs
More Than Expected (16 minutes)

As you watch the video, use the following outline to take notes on anything that stands out to you.

In our lives there are moments that we feel compelled to do something extravagant for God, and things don't turn out like we expect.

Jesus had performed many miracles, but raising Lazarus from the dead threatened the religious institutions and Roman Empire like no other.

The beautiful scent poured out, filling the house, permeating everyone's nostrils.

This is a breathtaking portrait of a woman who has been captivated by Jesus and cannot contain it any longer.

Mary is met with contempt for her extravagance.

As we live lives marked by extravagant acts of love, generosity, and worship, we should not be surprised by the critics. If anything, Mary's story teaches us we should expect them.

GROUP DISCUSSION QUESTIONS (30–45 minutes)

1. Consider what you learned about this beautiful miracle in the life of Lazarus from the Afterhours personal studies or on the video. What caught your attention or stood out most to you?

Captivated by Jesus

2. Read John 12:1–11. What do you think compelled Mary to use the alabaster jar in the beautiful way that she did?

NOTABLE
Respectable Jewish women always kept their hair up in public. To allow one's hair to flow freely was the sign of an immoral woman. Despite this cultural taboo, Mary lets down her hair with reckless abandon in this beautiful expression of adoration.

3. If you could question Mary about her extravagant and beautiful act, what would you want to know?

How do you imagine Mary's answers to your questions might impact your own relationship with Christ?

4. Read John 11:2. Why do you think Mary is introduced as having anointed the Lord before she actually anoints the Lord in this chapter?

Why do you think John's Gospel adds the detail about Mary wiping Jesus' feet with her hair? What do Mary's actions reveal about her attitude toward Jesus and their relationship?

What Have I Done?

5. What is a contemporary example of an extravagant display that would be comparable to Mary's act?

How might this contemporary example be viewed or even misinterpreted by others?

6. Have you ever given an extravagant gift or act of service to someone or to God and then second-guessed yourself, wondering, *What have I done?* What made you second-guess yourself?

7. This story suggests that extravagant devotion and generosity toward Jesus often will be misunderstood or even criticized. When have you found this to be true in your own life?

8. Are there any areas in which you find yourself quick to question, judge, or criticize those who give God something extravagant?

QUOTABLE

"Like Judas, we may ridicule Mary for her act of extravagance, which costs her a great deal—not only in terms of losing her savings but also in terms of losing face. How impractical! How outlandish and wasteful! But at times authentic worship will appear as impractical, as outlandish and as wasteful as it does here—just like God's grace, which is poured out lavishly on unworthy sinners like Mary, you, and me."[28]

—Paul Louis Metzger

Unable to Hold Back

9. Are there any areas in which you're holding back from offering something extravagant to God because of something that has happened in the past? If so, describe.

10. In what ways has God been extending an invitation to give yourself to him in a greater measure? How can you be more intentional about giving yourself extravagantly and lavishly to God in worship this week?

Mary's beautiful expression of worship didn't just challenge onlookers thousands of years ago but still challenges us today. It invites us to reflect on how we worship, what we sacrifice out of our love for Christ, and what we receive from him in response.

BONUS ACTIVITY

To learn more about the artist behind "Autumn Dancers" featured in the introduction of session ten, check out Lindsay Hoekstra's site at: www.lindsayhoekstra.com.

CLOSE IN PRAYER

Ask God to:

- Reveal any times when you may have felt disappointment or hurt from a well-intentioned offering.
- Give you his perspective on your act of worship and heal any areas of hurt.
- Reveal any times when you may have been critical of other people's worship or offering.
- Forgive you.

JUMPSTART

To prepare for the next group session, read John 18–19 and tackle the Afterhours personal studies.

Afterhours Personal Studies

Dive deeper into John's Gospel by engaging in these five personal studies. If you only have time for one, choose Day Five, which will prepare you specifically for the next session.

DAY ONE: Entering Jerusalem

JOHN 12:12–50

After raising Lazarus from the dead and being anointed by Mary for his own burial, Jesus now makes his triumphant entry into Jerusalem. The much anticipated Messiah arrives, and crowds of eager worshipers greet him by crying out, "Hosanna!" The word *Hosanna* can be translated "Save us!" or "Give us salvation now!" The shouts of those in the crowds echo the words of Psalm 118:26. The crowds also greet Jesus with palm branches in their hands. These branches were often used as part of the processions at the Feast of Tabernacles as well as to display Jewish patriotism. The people's use of palm branches to announce Jesus' arrival in Jerusalem suggests they were ready to accept him as the long-awaited Messiah, their king.

1. Read John 12:12–19. What do the details of Jesus' entry disclose about the way he is revealing himself as the Messiah? (*Hint:* See Zechariah 9:9 and Psalm 118:26.)

2. Read John 12:20–36. Why do you think Jesus goes to such great lengths to point people toward glorifying God? (*Hint:* See John 8:54; 13:31; 14:13.)

Think back over the last day or two. In what ways did your words, thoughts, or actions bring glory to God?

If you have trouble thinking of an example, consider any missed opportunities you may have had. How might you use a similar situation to glorify God in the future?

3. The world views death as the end, the ultimate loss, but through Scripture we see death as a new beginning and something through which we gain even more intimate access to God. What does Jesus specifically teach us about his death in this passage?

NOTABLE

John often uses the word *hour* to refer to the time of Jesus' crucifixion (i.e., John 12:23).

4. Read John 12:37–50. John's Gospel draws on Isaiah 6:10 and Isaiah 53:1 to explain how our hearts are hardened toward God. What happens to a person's spiritual senses when he or she refuses to obey or honor God?

   Are there any areas or relationships in your family, community, church, or workplace where you've become hardhearted?

5. Religious leaders and others in Jesus' day lived for the praise of people rather than the praise of God (John 12:43). In what ways have you been tempted to love the praise of people more than the praise of God?

6. Even after all of the rejection and criticism, Jesus still invites people to embrace the light, reject the darkness, and listen to his voice. Jesus invites people to eternal life. He longs to restore the relationship between people and God if they will simply respond to the invitation. What does this reveal about Jesus' heart for people?

   In what ways do you recognize Jesus' unending invitation in your own life?

Spend some time asking God to reveal any areas in your life where your heart has grown hard toward him. Ask God to soften your heart and allow the power of his truth to transform you.

DAY TWO: The Last Supper

JOHN 13

Before the Passover, Jesus shares an unforgettable meal with his followers in which he both washes their feet and exposes the one who will betray him. Through John 13 and the upcoming handful of chapters, we're given the opportunity to listen in on an intimate conversation between Jesus and his closest followers as well as watch how he interacts with them. These are some of the most tender and beautiful exchanges between Jesus and his disciples.

1. Read John 13:1–20. What does the passage reveal about why Jesus took on the duties of a slave or servant—washing the disciples' feet—during their final hours together?

   How does Jesus' act of washing the disciples' feet demonstrate the attitude he wants us to have toward others?

   In what situation or relationship is it most challenging for you right now to consider humbling yourself as a way of serving others?

NOTABLE

John's account of the Last Supper differs from the other Gospels. John notes the final supper is the night before instead of the night of the Passover. John doesn't mention the securing or preparation of the upper room, but includes the scene of the foot washing as well as the account of Judas' betrayal. In addition, John lacks the Eucharistic language or detailed description of Holy Communion found in the other Gospels.

2. When it comes to having a servant heart, how would you describe your behavior toward various people in your life: for example, your family; people you know at school, work, or in your daily activities; members of your church or small group; your neighborhood or community? Place an X on the following continuums to indicate your response.

With my family, I behave like . . .

A Humble Servant   Royalty

With people I know at school, work, or in my daily activities, I behave like . . .

A Humble Servant   Royalty

With people in my church or small group, I behave like . . .

A Humble Servant   Royalty

With people in my neighborhood or community, I behave like . . .

A Humble Servant   Royalty

As you review your responses on the continuums, how would you describe the degree to which your relationships demonstrate a servant heart?

3. Although we can't go around offering to wash the feet of everyone we know, we can make small decisions every day to serve others. What equivalents of foot washing might you practice with the people in your life? Write down one or two ideas for each group listed below.

In my home or with extended family members

In my school, workplace, or other daily activities

In my church or small group

In my neighborhood or community

> **NOTABLE**
> The three moments when Jesus is noted as being troubled in spirit
> are all found in John's Gospel—John 11:33, 12:27, and 13:21—and all
> illustrate a response to human suffering and death.

4. Read John 13:21–38. Why do you think Jesus selected Judas as a disciple when he knew Judas would pilfer money and eventually betray him?

5. Jesus says that people will know we are his disciples by our love for one another (John 13:35). Think back over the last day or two. In what ways have you struggled with the command to love one another?

Spend some time asking God to expand your heart for service. Ask for a special sensitivity to those around you who are in need as well as for wisdom in how to respond with the love of God.

DAY THREE: Final Words of Comfort

JOHN 14–15

One can only imagine what Judas felt as he looked into Jesus' eyes as the Son of God tenderly washed between his toes. Only a few moments later, Jesus dismisses Judas from dinner to do what he had been planning for some time—betray his rabbi. The rest of the disciples finish the meal listening to Jesus' words of comfort and challenge.

1. Read John 14:1–31. How does Jesus comfort his followers throughout this passage? How do Jesus' words comfort you?

SCRIPTURE	HOW DOES JESUS COMFORT HIS FOLLOWERS?	HOW DO JESUS' WORDS COMFORT YOU?
John 14:1-4	*Example: He instructs his disciples not to be troubled and assures them that he is preparing a place for them.*	*Example: God is also preparing a place for me!*
John 14:12-13		
John 14:16		
John 14:18		
John 14:27		
John 14:29		

One of the most important sources of comfort to the disciples is the Holy Spirit—who is called Counselor (or Helper, NASB) in John 14:16, 26. Jesus promises that the Holy Spirit will help the disciples to remember all that he taught them (v. 26). Remembering was an important facet of faith throughout the Old Testament as well. People were to remember the words God spoke to them in the past. Some even built pillars or rock altars to commemorate God's activity among them.

2. How do memories of God's past activity in your life impact your ability to trust God in the present?

NOTABLE

Shalom, the Hebrew word for "peace" used in John 14:27, communicates much more than a lack of conflict. *Shalom* suggests the idea of the blessing that overflows when one is in right relationship with God.

After describing himself as the way, truth, and life (John 14:6), Jesus goes on to reveal himself as the true vine (John 15:1). Since, according to John 14:31, Jesus had left the upper room, some scholars believe that when Jesus delivered his teaching on the vines he was either near the golden vine image that decorated the main entrance of the temple or in a nearby field where vines were planted.

3. Read John 15:1–11. *Abide* means "to remain, continue, stay; to have one's abode, dwell, reside; or continue in a particular condition, attitude, or relationship."[29] Jesus commands his disciples to "remain [abide] in me" (John 15:4) rather than commanding them to be fruitful. Which is more challenging for you —to abide in Christ or to do good works for Christ? Why?

4. Read John 15:12–27. Most of us won't be required to literally lay down our lives for someone we love, but we can choose to make personal sacrifices for the sake of others. How has a friend or family member laid down his or her life for you by putting your needs first?

How did this sacrifice impact you and your relationship with this person?

5. How have you laid down your life for someone else recently by putting his or her needs first?

How did your sacrifice impact the other person and your relationship with that person?

Spend some time praying about what it looks like for you to abide in Jesus in the midst of your daily schedule and routine. Ask God for the strength and grace to dwell or reside in Christ.

DAY FOUR: Jesus' Final Promise and Prayer

JOHN 16–17

Jesus continues to inform the disciples about what's going to happen so they aren't caught unaware. The disciples should anticipate hostility from the religious establishment but also know that God's Spirit is with them even in the midst of fiery trials.

1. Read John 16:1–15. This passage teaches that the Holy Spirit convicts the world of three things—sin, righteousness, and judgment. How does each of these convictions reveal Jesus as the Messiah, the Son of God? How have you experienced each conviction of the Holy Spirit in your own life?

HOW THE HOLY SPIRIT CONVICTS THE WORLD	HOW THIS CONVICTION REVEALS JESUS AS THE MESSIAH	HOW I HAVE EXPERIENCED THE CONVICTION OF THE HOLY SPIRIT
Sin		
Righteousness		
Judgment		

> **NOTABLE**
>
> In his final words to his followers before his arrest, Jesus is abundantly clear that the road before them will not be easy. They will encounter persecution, trials, and challenges. We should not be surprised when we face "fiery ordeals" (1 Peter 4:12 NASB).

2. How is the promised work of the Holy Spirit explained differently in John 16:13–15 than John 14:26?

How have you experienced the Holy Spirit working in your own life?

3. Read John 16:16–33. Why do you think the disciples were confused by Jesus' use of the phrase "a little while" (vv. 16–17)?

The disciples became more concerned with the timing of the promise than the promise itself. In what ways do believers today get distracted by the timing of God's promises rather than the actual promises?

In what ways do you find yourself distracted by the timing of God's promises rather than the actual promises?

NOTABLE

John 16:22-24 highlights a new point of connection between the disciples and Jesus. Though they've made requests of both God and Jesus, now they're to ask God in Jesus' name. The disciples will encounter difficulties, but God will supply joy in abundance. The joy the disciples will experience is made possible through prayer.

In John 16:31 (NASB), Jesus asks, "Do you now believe?" His question highlights a message reiterated throughout John's Gospel. The book was written so that people would believe. Now Jesus himself is asking the question, "Do you now believe?" Jesus then proceeds to pray for himself and his disciples.

4. Read John 17:1–26. What is the one request Jesus makes for himself (v. 1)?

Why do you think Jesus makes this request?

NOTABLE

Moses (Numbers 11:15), Elijah (1 Kings 19:4), and Jonah (Jonah 4:3, 8) all asked God to take them out of the world. God denied all of their requests. In John 17:15, Jesus prays that his disciples would not be taken from the world, but remain in it—set apart as God's people and protected from the evil one.

5. What does Jesus' prayer reveal about his desire for his followers—including you?

6. On the evening of Jesus' arrest, he does not pray for immediate concerns but long-term issues that his disciples will face in the future. Do you tend to pray for immediate concerns or long-term concerns? Place an X on the continuum below to describe your response.

I Pray for Immediate Concerns   I Pray for Long-term Concerns

If a balanced prayer life includes having a conversation with God about both immediate and long-term concerns, what kinds of things would be on your prayer list? Write three or four items in each column below.

MY IMMEDIATE CONCERNS	MY LONG-TERM CONCERNS

Spend some time asking God to increase your awareness of the presence of the Holy Spirit in your life as both a source of conviction and a source of comfort.

DAY FIVE: A Double Betrayal

JOHN 18:1–27

Judas is the name most of us think of first when it comes to Jesus' betrayal. John's Gospel reveals in detail that not one but two of Jesus' disciples betrayed him. John 18 places the accounts back to back, providing a setting to compare the two betrayals and how each betrayer responded.

NOTABLE

In John 18:4–5 (NASB), Jesus asks the Roman cohort and religious leaders, "Whom do you seek?" "Jesus of Nazareth," they answer. Jesus replies, "I am he"—a statement reflective of the many "I am" statements found throughout John that reveal Jesus' relationship with God.

1. Read John 18:1–11. What do you think the disciples first thought when they saw Judas with the Roman cohort and religious leaders carrying lanterns, torches, and weapons?

   If you had been among the disciples, what would have been your reaction?

   What do you imagine ran through Jesus' mind when he saw Judas?

2. Read Matthew 26:47–50. How does Matthew's account of Jesus' betrayal differ from John's? What does each writer emphasize about Judas' betrayal?

3. Read Matthew 27:1–10. After the betrayal, Judas feels remorse. How does he handle the remorse?

Do you think the story of Judas had to end the way it did? Why or why not?

NOTABLE

According to John 18:6, when Jesus said, "I am he," the soldiers fell to the ground. This is reminiscent of scenes throughout the Old Testament where people responded to the power and revelation of God by falling on their faces (Genesis 17:3; Joshua 5:14; Ezekiel 1:28).

4. Read John 18:12–27. How is Peter's betrayal of Jesus similar to and different from Judas' betrayal?

In your own life, have you ever betrayed Jesus? How did your betrayal impact your relationship with Christ?

5. Read John 21:15–21. Why do you think Jesus goes out of his way to speak to Peter and remind him of his purpose, calling, and future?

6. What insights can you learn from Judas and Peter about sin and temptation in your life?

What insights can you learn from Judas and Peter about redemption and restoration in your life?

Spend some time prayerfully asking God to reveal ways in which you have either betrayed or denied the work of God in your life. Ask for forgiveness as well as the grace to walk in faithfulness.

Mistakes That Refine Instead of Define

John 18-19

Moral principles are vital, yet so often we have to drive ourselves to do what is right. Beauty, on the other hand, haunts us. It draws and compels and gives. . . . I might respond to God as a great commander-in-chief but I could not give myself to him as the goal of all my longing and my supreme delight.[30]

—RICHARD HARRIES

Just because God is beautiful and God is perfect does not mean that God's beauty can only be reflected in perfection. Rather, God showcases the beauty of his work on broken and imperfect canvases. Some of God's most beautiful work is on display in the lives of those whose pasts are most messed up, whose situations seemed beyond repair.

We all have circumstances and situations in life that we look back on and think, *I wish I had handled things differently. I wish had been more honest. I wish I had been more courageous. I wish I had been the one to speak up.* Yet the question we must all face is whether we will allow our mistakes to define us or to refine us. As we submit ourselves to God's work in our lives we can find that our weaknesses and failures become places for the glory of God to infuse, heal, and invite us into wholeness.

GETTING STARTED: Select One (10–15 minutes)

Experiential Activity: Imagining the Flavors of Eden

What you'll need:

- Humorous and engaging photos or images that portray failure
- Photocopies of the images, or a laptop and video projector to display the images

1. Visit www.failblog.org, a website that allows people to upload images of various failures—many of which are failures in communication. (*Note:* Since this website is open to anyone uploading photos, be aware that some language and images may not be appropriate for distributing in the group. Discretion advised.)
2. Select four or five humorous, engaging, and thought-provoking failure images and print them out.
3. Pass the images around the group.
4. Discuss the following questions:
   - What does each image reveal about the person who failed?
   - Do you find the failure funny? Why or why not?
   - Which failure causes you to have the most compassion on the person who failed? Why?

Icebreaker Question

*If you're not doing the experiential activity, choose **one** of the following sets of questions to begin your discussion.*

- If you had one do-over in an area of your life—professional, relational, or spiritual—what would you choose? Why?
- What tends to be your response to personal failure? How does your response change when it's someone else who has failed?
- Use your imagination for a moment. If you had the opportunity to ask the disciple Peter, "What is your most regrettable moment?" how do you think he would answer?

VIDEO ELEVEN: Mistakes that Refine
Instead of Define (14 minutes)

As you watch the video, use the following outline to take notes on anything that stands out to you.

Why didn't I speak up?

Once Christ is arrested, we get a different glimpse of Peter.

Jesus is questioned by the authorities and denies nothing, while Peter is questioned by strangers and denies everything.

On that morning, Peter felt defeated not by armies or authorities, but by himself.

Peter's denial of Jesus does not define him; it refined him.

I can't go back and make things happen in a different way than they did in that room with those religious leaders that day. But I can go forward.

GROUP DISCUSSION QUESTIONS (30–45 minutes)

1. Consider what you learned about this beautiful portrait of restoration in the life of Peter from the Afterhours personal studies or on the video. What caught your attention or stood out most to you?

Why Didn't I Speak Up?

2. Have you ever been in a situation where you wish you had spoken up about your faith but instead remained silent? Briefly describe the situation and why you chose not to say anything.

   If you could go back into that situation and say something, what would you say?

3. Read John 18:12–27. Why do you think Peter didn't speak up and admit to being a follower of Jesus?

Mistakes that Define

4. What emotions do you think Peter felt when he heard the sound of a rooster announcing the dawn of a new day?

Which of those emotions can you relate to in your own moments of failure?

5. Read Luke 22:54–62. How does Luke's account of Peter's denial differ from John's account?

6. Luke describes Jesus turning and looking at Peter (Luke 22:61). What do you think was communicated to Peter through that glance?

Mistakes that Refine

7. Pair up with another person. Take turns reading aloud to each other the passages listed on the chart that follows. After each passage, briefly discuss what it teaches about how God looks at our failures and mistakes and how this truth encourages you. Briefly note your responses in the space provided.

SCRIPTURE	WHAT IT TEACHES ABOUT HOW GOD LOOKS AT OUR FAILURES AND MISTAKES	HOW THIS TRUTH ENCOURAGES ME
Psalm 73:26		
Romans 8:1–2		
Romans 8:35–39		
1 John 1:9		
John 21:15–22		

8. How would you describe the difference between being *defined* by a failure and being *refined* by a failure?

9. What role does God play in the difference between being refined versus being defined by a mistake?

10. How have you seen God play a role in your own life when it comes to being refined rather than defined by a mistake?

We all can look back on times when we wish we had responded differently. Though we can't go back and change the past, we can move forward. We are given countless opportunities not only to share our faith but to live it out, bearing witness to God's redemption.

BONUS ACTIVITY

To learn more about the artist behind "Solo" featured in the introduction of session eleven, check out David Warmenhoven's site at: www.warmenhovenart.blogspot.com.

CLOSE IN PRAYER

Ask God to:

- Reveal any moments from the past that may have defined you instead of refined you to become more Christlike.
- Make you receptive to the Holy Spirit's work, especially in areas of your life that need to be illuminated by truth or experience healing.
- Give you the courage to respond differently in areas where you have failed in the past.

JUMPSTART

To prepare for the next group session, read John 20:1–18 and tackle the Afterhours personal studies.

Afterhours Personal Studies

Dive deeper into John's Gospel by engaging in these five personal studies. If you only have time for one, choose Day Five, which will prepare you specifically for the next session.

DAY ONE: Standing Trial Unjustly

JOHN 18:12-40

Jesus is given two different trials. He stands before both Jewish and Roman judges. John's Gospel is the only one to mention that Jesus appears before Annas. Why does he go before Annas when it's his son-in-law, Caiaphas, who actually holds the position of high priest? Some scholars believe that because the appointment for high priest was for life (Numbers 35:25), Annas may have been seen as the real high priest or the one with more experience, age, and authority.

Jesus is questioned in an informal manner. Jewish law required witnesses to be present in a formal trial, but since none are mentioned, the questioning is probably not official. The turn of events suggests that the case should have been dismissed as a mistrial, but instead a series of events lead to Jesus' execution.

1. Read John 18:12–24. What does Jesus reveal when questioned about his disciples and teaching?

Why do you think one of the officers strikes Jesus? (*Hint:* See Exodus 22:28.)

John's Gospel only briefly mentions that Annas sent Jesus to Caiaphas, the high priest of the year. Before Jesus could stand before a Roman court, the charges against him had to be made by the official Jewish priest. Only then is Jesus taken into the headquarters of the Romans to stand trial before Pilate.

Jews who walked into the house of any Gentile were deemed unclean and unable to celebrate the Passover. Thus, the Jews refused to walk into the Praetorium where Jesus stood trial before the Roman ruler Pilate.

NOTABLE

Barabbas' name can be translated as "son of the father." This phrase parallels the way John's Gospel describes Jesus throughout the text. The people literally chose between two different sons of the father.

2. Do you think it's hypocritical that the Jewish leaders refuse to enter the Praetorium? Why or why not?

3. Read John 18:25–40. What is Pilate's overall response to the religious leaders' charges against Jesus?

How does Pilate try to set Jesus free? Why do his efforts fail?

John's Gospel repeatedly uses the word *king* to describe Jesus. In fact, when Jesus calls his first disciples (John 1:49), Nathanael makes the initial declaration that Jesus is not only the Son of God, but the king of Israel. In the sixth chapter of John, when Jesus perceives the people are going to come and take him by force in order to instate him as king, he retreats to a quiet mountainside. When Jesus enters Jerusalem on a donkey, he is greeted with the title "king of Israel."

QUOTABLE

"In a scene full of dramatic power John pictures for us the lowly majesty of Jesus confronting the proud majesty of Rome's representative. Subtly, but very definitely, John brings out the supreme royalty of Jesus. He will be slain, but this does not detract from his majesty."[32]

—Leon Morris

4. Jesus' kingship is questioned and mocked throughout his arrest, trial, and crucifixion. Why do you think Pilate called Jesus "the king of the Jews" when requesting his release (v. 39)?

Why would the Jewish people react so negatively to this title for Jesus?

5. What in this passage suggests that God is fully in control throughout Jesus' trials?

Jesus' trial is marked by injustice. No witnesses provide testimony of Jesus' guilt nor does Caiaphas. Though the Jews call Jesus a criminal, there's not any proof. Pilate finds no basis of a crime that Jesus has committed. Yet despite all this, Jesus is found guilty based on nothing more than political maneuvering.

6. What types of situations make you question whether God is fully in control?

What does it mean for you to trust God or commit yourself to God's care even in the midst of life's most severe trials?

Spend time reflecting on areas of your life that feel completely out of control. Ask God to give you grace, strength, and faith in these areas and to wholly trust that God is in control.

DAY TWO: Innocent Punishable by Death

JOHN 19:1–15

Following Jesus' trial, Pilate decides to have Jesus scourged and then to release him in the hope that this will appease the Jews. In addition to the scourging, the soldiers seem to take pleasure in harassing Jesus.

1. Read John 19:1–3. How do the soldiers mock Jesus?

Why do you think the soldiers were so committed to humiliating Jesus?

2. Read John 19:4–15. How does Pilate's approach and attitude toward Jesus differ from that of the soldiers?

3. How would you describe the Jews' attitude toward Jesus?

NOTABLE

Some scholars believe the day of preparation during Passover refers to the day in which the lambs are being prepared for execution at the temple. Thus, Jesus' preparation for crucifixion parallels the preparation of the Passover lambs.

4. Briefly review your responses to questions 1–3. How do you see the attitudes of Pilate, the soldiers, and the Jews demonstrated in people's attitudes toward Jesus today?

Pilate

The soldiers

The Jews

In what ways, if any, have these attitudes sometimes characterized your own response to Jesus?

5. In what areas of your own life have you discovered your heart becoming hard toward God? Toward others?

Spend some time in prayer reflecting on your attitude toward God. Ask the Holy Spirit to illuminate any areas where God wants to soften your heart.

DAY THREE: Jesus' Final Words

JOHN 19:16-30

John's account of Jesus' death differs from the other Gospels. Details are specifically chosen to highlight certain beliefs, moods, and relationships. Instead of a cry on the cross asking why God has forsaken him, Jesus declares that it's finished. This portrait suggests that Jesus is in control from beginning to end. Jesus is not being forced to die; he is choosing to give up his own life.

The Gospel of John testifies that Jesus is given over to the Jews to be crucified and forced to carry his own cross to the place of his execution. Pilate writes an inscription for Jesus that declared "Jesus the Nazarene, the King of the Jews" in three different languages so that all who could read would understand. The religious leaders protest the inscription, but Pilate refuses to make any adjustments or to take it down.

1. Look up the following passages and write down Jesus' final words from each crucifixion account:

SCRIPTURE	JESUS' FINAL WORDS
Matthew 27:33–50	
Mark 15:22–41	
Luke 23:33–49	
John 19:16–30	

2. Which of Jesus' statements impacts you the most? Why?

3. What do Jesus' statements reveal about Jesus' identity and mission?

NOTABLE

Jesus' final cry—"It is finished"—in John's Gospel are not words of concession or defeat, but a powerful declaration that Jesus has triumphantly fulfilled his mission.

4. Why do you think John's Gospel notes that Jesus expressed concern for his mother?

What do you think Mary felt as she watched these events unfold (Luke 2:19)?

QUOTABLE

"Therefore I will give him a portion among the great, and he will divide the spoils with the strong, because he poured out his life unto death, and was numbered with the transgressors. For he bore the sin of many, and made intercession for the transgressors."

—Isaiah 53:12

5. In what ways was Jesus dead to the things of this world long before he ever hung on a cross?

6. In what area of your life might God be calling you to take up your cross and die to your own desires?

The prospect of dying to anything can be frightening, but death always precedes new life. What new life do you hope might emerge from accepting God's invitation to die to yourself?

Spend some time asking God to give you the strength to respond with a sense of joy and expectation to anything God may be calling you to die to.

DAY FOUR: Jesus' Burial

JOHN 19:31-42

The Romans often allowed the corpse of a person who had been crucified to remain on the cross until it was devoured by birds and wild animals. But the Jews did not want bodies to remain on the cross for the holy day, so they sped along their removal. The soldiers break the legs of a criminal being executed alongside Jesus so he can no longer lift himself up to breathe. Noting that Jesus is dead, they leave his bones unbroken. To confirm Jesus' death, a soldier pierces his body with a spear. The Scripture notes that blood and water flowed as a result (John 19:34).

1. Read John 19:31–42. Why is the detail of Jesus' bones remaining unbroken so significant? (*Hint:* See Exodus 12:46; Numbers 9:12; Psalm 34:20.)

NOTABLE

Some scholars believe the water and blood that burst from Jesus' side are symbolic of the Lord's Supper (blood) and baptism (water).

After Jesus' body is removed from the cross, Joseph of Arimathea suddenly appears and disappears from John's Gospel. The one act he is known for is caring for Jesus' body. Though many followers flee after Jesus' death, Joseph courageously steps forward to ask for the remains.

2. What do the following passages reveal about Joseph of Arimathea?

PASSAGE	JOSEPH OF ARIMATHEA
Mark 15:43	
Luke 23:50	
Matthew 27:57	

In what ways, if any, have you tried to keep your relationship with Jesus a secret as Joseph of Arimathea did two thousand years ago?

3. Does Nicodemus' appearance in John 19 surprise you? Why or why not?

4. What does Nicodemus' appearance suggest that he now believes (following his initial meeting with Jesus at night in John 3)?

5. In your own spiritual life, would you describe yourself as a daytime follower (like the disciples) or a nighttime follower like Nicodemus? Explain.

Spend some time asking God to give you more courage to express and share your faith in your everyday life.

DAY FIVE: An Empty Tomb and an Unlikely Witness

JOHN 20:1-18

Though Joseph of Arimathea and Nicodemus provide a tomb and spices for the body, one can only imagine the pain and anguish, confusion and fear all the followers of Jesus feel following his death. The source of their hope is gone. Now what?

John's Gospel describes an unlikely character by the name of Mary Magdalene approaching the tomb. The only other time John's Gospel mentions Mary Magdalene is John 19:25 when she appears at the cross.

1. Read John 20:1–18 and then look up the passages listed below. What does each one reveal about Mary Magdalene?

SCRIPTURE	MARY MAGDALENE
Matthew 27:55–56	
Mark 15:40–41	
Luke 8:1–3	

NOTABLE

Stealing a body was considered a horrible offense in Jewish culture. Emperor Claudius eventually made grave robbing a capital crime punishable by death.

2. Why do you think that of all the people Jesus could have revealed himself to after the resurrection he chose to reveal himself to Mary Magdalene?

What might this reveal about Jesus' mission and identity?

3. John's Gospel notes details about how the linens from Jesus' body were discovered. What do the linens (vv. 6–7) suggest about the scene and what may have happened to Jesus' body?

4. Of all of the questions Jesus could have asked Mary Magdalene, why do you think that he asks her, "Who is it you are looking for?"

   What does the first thing Mary Magdalene says when she recognizes Jesus reveal about her relationship with Jesus?

5. Scholars debate why Jesus told Mary Magdalene not to hold onto him. Some believe Jesus is telling Mary to let go of him so she can go and tell the disciples. Others suggest that Jesus is telling Mary that she can't hold onto Jesus in his current form, because he has yet to come again. The relationship is changing and Mary can't cling to the past. Still others suggest that Jesus is instructing Mary to let go of him in his physical form because Jesus is going to send the Holy Spirit. Why do you think Jesus told Mary Magdalene not to hold onto him?

   What do you think Jesus was trying to communicate?

   What would your reaction have been if Jesus had revealed himself to you as he did to Mary?

6. What is your response to the risen Christ?

Who is the first person that comes to mind when you think about sharing the good news of Christ's resurrection with someone?

Spend time reflecting on John 20:1–18. Prayerfully imagine what it would be like to be the first person to the tomb. What would you expect to see and encounter? What would be your response to the risen Christ? Thank Jesus not only for his sacrifice but for the resurrection. Ask God to make the resurrection even more alive in your own heart.

The Hope and Healing of Resurrection

John 20-21

In one of the New Testament's greatest claims, the kingdoms of this world are to become the kingdom of God, so the beauty of this world will be enfolded in the beauty of God— and not just the beauty of God himself, but the beauty which, because God is the creator par excellence, he will create when the present world is rescued, healed, restored, and completed.[33]

—N. T. WRIGHT

Of all the portraits of Jesus throughout John's Gospel, perhaps none is more stunning than the resurrection. This moment invites us to believe that Jesus is who he said he was—the very Son of God who walked the earth, laid down his life, and returned to the Father. The resurrection is an invitation to embrace the beauty of God through the person of Jesus by believing in him.

Throughout the Gospel of John, we see again and again that Jesus knows his mission. At times, he hints to his followers about "the hour" of his death. At other times, Jesus takes a much more direct route in preparing his disciples for the events that are about to unfold. Even in his arrest, trial, and crucifixion, Jesus displays that he is who he has said he's been all along. Jesus' death is not the end of the story!

GETTING STARTED: Select One (10–15 minutes)

Experiential Activity: Images of the Resurrection

What you'll need:

- Well-known and/or unknown images of the resurrection
- Photocopies of the images, or a laptop and video projector to display the images

1. Google "famous resurrection artwork" to find images of the resurrection. One site that is helpful is www.bible-art.info/resurrection.htm. Consider looking at Rembrandt's *The Resurrection*, El Greco's *The Resurrection*, and Frederick Hart's *Christ Rising*, among others.
2. Pass the images around the group.
3. Discuss the following questions:
   - Which image do you find most compelling? Why?
   - What mood did the artist capture?
   - What emotions are conveyed through each person's expression?
   - What does the artwork communicate about Jesus' relationship to his followers and his relationship to God?

Icebreaker Question

*If you're not doing the experiential activity, choose **one** of the following sets of questions to begin your discussion.*

- Have you ever celebrated Lent—the forty days before Easter devoted to penitence, prayer, and self-denial—in order to prepare for the resurrection? If so, describe your experience and what you learned.
- Other than Easter, what seasons or situations remind you of the resurrection of Jesus? Why is it important to reflect on the resurrection in your own spiritual journey?
- Have you ever visited the Holy Land? If so, what was your most meaningful experience? If you haven't visited the Holy Land but were given the opportunity, where is the one place you'd want to go? Why?

VIDEO TWELVE: The Hope and Healing
of Resurrection (16 minutes)

As you watch the video, use the following outline to take notes on anything that stands out to you.

Stepping inside the tomb, dark and cold, I was struck by the fact there's no one there.

The disciples head back home to try to wrap their minds and hearts around all they've seen and experienced. Mary just sits by the tomb.

The Son of God who created the skies, formed the mountains, and unleashed the solar system, is now mistaken for a gardener.

Sometimes all it takes is one word from God and everything changes.

The invitation to know Jesus is an invitation to believe in him.

The same power of God that raised Jesus from the dead isn't what was but what is.

GROUP DISCUSSION QUESTIONS (30–45 minutes)

1. Based on the video teaching or the Afterhours personal studies, what have you learned from the beautiful portrait of resurrection in the life of Jesus and his encounters after he rose from the dead? What caught your attention or stood out most to you?

NOTABLE

The Gospel of John's account of the resurrection is different than any of the other Gospels. John's Gospel tells stories others do not and omits stories that others tell, but still celebrates the resurrection and morning discovery of the empty tomb.

2. What range of emotions do you think Jesus' followers experienced after his death and before the resurrection? What emotions would you experience if you were in the same situation?

The Resurrection Power of Jesus

3. Read John 20:1–18. What is significant about Mary Magdalene being the first person to discover the empty tomb? What is John's Gospel trying to communicate about the relationship between Jesus and women?

NOTABLE

A woman's testimony was not considered evidence in court. Only men's testimonies were considered. Jesus tells Mary—a woman whose testimony doesn't count—to go tell the disciples of Jesus' resurrection. The very first evangelist of the risen Christ is a woman! John's Gospel esteems women and the role they play as children of God.

4. Throughout the Gospel of John, many people have misinterpreted Jesus' teachings and identity.
- Jesus' body is misinterpreted as an earthly temple (John 2:20).
- Nicodemus misinterprets what it means to be born again or from above (John 3:4).
- The woman at the well misinterprets Jesus' promise of living water (John 4:13–14).
- Spiritual food is confused with regular food (John 4:33).
- Receiving Christ's Spirit is confused with eating Jesus' body and drinking Jesus' blood (John 6:52).
- Jesus' leaving is misinterpreted as Jesus killing himself (John 8:22).
- Spiritual bondage is misinterpreted as physical slavery (John 8:33).

What misunderstanding have you had in the past about God? What opened your eyes or ears to understanding?

A Change in Perspective

5. With one word Jesus breaks through Mary's grief-induced fog and enables her to see what's really going on. Have you ever sensed God communicating to you in a way that changed everything? If so, describe.

How does God most often break through your spiritual fog (for example: in the details of daily life, in spiritual conversations with others, through personal Bible study or prayer, etc.)?

6. Read John 20:19–31. Use your imagination. Where you do think Thomas was when Jesus appeared to the others? (*Note:* Be creative and even humorous in your answers—such as he was out fishing for the big one!)

Thomas spent years with Jesus witnessing miracles and listening to teaching, yet he refuses to believe. What are some things about God that are still hard for you to believe or wrap your mind around?

QUOTABLE

"The empty tomb never resists honest investigation. A lobotomy is not a prerequisite of discipleship. Following Christ demands faith, but not blind faith. 'Come and see,' the angel invites. Shall we?"[34]

—Max Lucado

7. Jesus' appearance after the resurrection is consistent with all he has promised, taught, and declared. What changes about being a follower of Jesus Christ after the resurrection?

The Call to Believe

8. In John 20:30–31, we are reminded of the purpose of John's Gospel. It's written so that people will believe that Jesus is the Christ. How has this study of John's Gospel impacted your view of Jesus or your relationship with Jesus?

QUOTABLE

"The goal of Jesus' coming into the world is that people come to God, know God, and believe in God."[35]

—Craig R. Koester

9. In what area of your life do you most long for new life?

How do you imagine things might change if you could experience the resurrection power of Christ in this area of your life?

10. As you reflect on the last six sessions you've spent studying John's Gospel, what have been some of the most meaningful insights or echoes that God has been speaking to you?

The empty tomb and the resurrection power of Christ calls us to life—whole, abundant life. Through his death, resurrection, and promise of imminent return we have the opportunity to live in a vibrant relationship with Jesus.

BONUS ACTIVITY
To learn more about the artist behind "For the Joy Set before Him" featured in the introduction of session twelve, check out Alexis Wilson's site at: www.alexis-art.com.

CLOSE IN PRAYER

Ask God to:

- Reveal the resurrection power in your life.
- Unleash healing and restoration into every area of life—including broken relationships, work situations, financial challenges, health struggles, etc.
- Draw people into the wonder of God's beauty in the person of Jesus Christ.

JUMPSTART

Tackle the Afterhours personal studies and consider organizing a final gathering for your group to connect, share a meal, and hang out. Thanks for spending these past twelve weeks digging deeper into the Bible to explore God's love and beauty in the books of Genesis and John.

SESSION TWELVE

Afterhours Personal Studies

Dive deeper into John's Gospel by engaging in these five personal studies.

DAY ONE: A Surprise Appearance among the Disciples

JOHN 20:19-31

Behind locked doors, the disciples are huddled together. Mary Magdalene has answered countless questions about what she saw, heard, and experienced at the garden tomb. Some of the disciples are probably wondering if what she said really happened. Simon Peter and another disciple (most likely John) confirmed the body was missing, but they never saw Jesus. Yet something about the passion and details of Mary Magdalene's story makes them want to believe it's true.

1. Read John 20:19–30. How does Jesus greet the disciples?

In what ways is this greeting consistent with Jesus' mission and identity? (*Hint:* See John 14:27 and 16:33.)

2. Why does Jesus breathe on the disciples?

What biblical images come to mind when you reflect on this scene? (*Hint:* See Genesis 2:7, John 1:33; John 3:34; John 14:17.)

NOTABLE

John doesn't use the noun *faith* (Greek: *pistis*) in his Gospel, but uses the verb *to believe* (Greek: *pisteuo*) almost a hundred times. John's Gospel remains focused on inviting readers to believe in Jesus.

3. Do you think Thomas' demand to see and touch Jesus' wounds is reasonable? Why or why not?

In what ways are Thomas' demands still prevalent today?

4. Why do you think Jesus reappears to the disciples and addresses Thomas' struggle with faith?

What does this reveal about Jesus' promise to make sure none are lost?

5. Jesus pursues Thomas. He specifically reveals himself to Thomas, inviting Thomas to touch his scars. In what ways has Jesus been pursuing you over the course of this study?

6. What evidence or reasoning convinces you to believe that Jesus rose from the dead?

What does the resurrection mean to you personally? How does your view of the resurrection impact your relationship with Christ?

Spend some time reflecting on the ways in which Jesus has personally made himself real to you. Ask Jesus to continue revealing himself to you in very personal, real, and meaningful ways that strengthen your faith. Keep an eye and ear open for the ways he may answer that prayer during the upcoming week.

DAY TWO: Jesus Hosts Breakfast on the Beach

JOHN 21:1–14

In the final chapter of the Gospel of John, Jesus appears unexpectedly to his disciples after a long night of fishing. There's something tender about this beautiful scene of Jesus meeting his disciples right where they are—on the edge of the lake—in order to share a meal.

1. Read John 21:1–14. In the midst of so much uncertainty, why do you think Peter decides to return to fishing?

   What do you return to when you face uncertainty in your own life?

NOTABLE

Peter is from Bethsaida, which can be translated in Hebrew as "house of fish."

2. What does Peter's response to hearing "it is the Lord" (vv. 7–8) reveal about Peter's own desire to know and follow Jesus?

3. The meal Jesus provides the disciples is not new to them. Where else has Jesus eaten the same meal with his followers? (*Hint:* See John 6:1–14.)

What memories do you think this meal invokes in the disciples?

4. The mention of a charcoal fire is only found in one other place in the New Testament. What happened the last time Peter found himself standing in front of a charcoal fire? (*Hint:* See John 18:18 NASB.)

5. Read Luke 5:1–11. What parallels do you see between the accounts of Jesus approaching the disciples on the lake of Gennesaret early in his ministry and Jesus approaching the disciples on the lake of Tiberias after the resurrection?

6. In what ways are you allowing Jesus to meet you where you are in your life right now?

Spend some time asking God to meet you right where you are in your relationships, personal life, and daily responsibilities. Be expectant for God's presence in your life.

DAY THREE: Jesus Challenges Peter

JOHN 21:15–25

After an unforgettable breakfast with Jesus on the beach, Jesus focuses on Peter. Just as Peter denied Jesus three times after his arrest, Jesus now reinstates Peter by asking him three questions.

1. Read John 21:15–25. Jesus asks Peter, "Do you truly love me more than these?" Considering the scene, what do you think "these" refers to?

NOTABLE
There are multiple words for "love" in Greek—two of which are *agape* and *phileo*. *Agape* expresses an unconditional, sacrificial love (like that of Christ for us). *Phileo* is a friendship-type love (think Phil-adelphia).

2. How does Jesus connect love and service in his interaction with Peter? How are love of God and service of God connected in your own faith journey?

3. How does Jesus give Peter a second chance?

What from the origins of Peter's name gives insight into Peter's purpose for the church? (*Hint:* See John 1:42.)

In what ways has God extended a second chance to you?

4. How does Peter's story encourage you?

How might you respond if Jesus were to call you by name and ask you, "_____, do you love me?"

What do you think Jesus might ask you to do for him as a sign of your love?

Spend some time prayerfully considering how God has been calling you to care for his flock. What opportunities has God been opening up for you to pour into the lives of others and make the journey of faith with them?

DAY FOUR: Life to the Fullest

As you've been reading John's Gospel, you may have noticed the frequent use of the word *life*. It appears more in this Gospel than in any other book in the New Testament. In fact, more than one fourth of all the mentions of *life* in the New Testament are found in John's Gospel.

1. Look up the passages in the following chart. What does each reveal about the "life" John's Gospel mentions?

SCRIPTURE	WHAT THIS PASSAGE REVEALS ABOUT "LIFE"
John 1:4	
John 3:16	
John 3:36	
John 5:21	
John 5:40	
John 6:35	
John 6:63	
John 8:12	
John 10:10	
John 10:17	
John 20:31	

These passages demonstrate that a relationship with Christ is the source of all life. In what ways have you discovered this to be true?

QUOTABLE

"Jesus can claim to be the resurrection and the life because he proclaims and embodies the Word of God that evokes faith. The integrity of his word will be demonstrated in a provisional way when he calls Lazarus from the tomb and in a definitive way when he lays down his own life through crucifixion and takes it up through the resurrection."[36]

—Craig R. Koester

2. In what ways have you looked for life, including abundant life, outside of Jesus? What has been the result?

3. What spiritual practices strengthen your relationship with Jesus and awaken you spiritually?

4. Which areas of your life would you like to fill so that you're overflowing with God's presence and abundant life?

Spend some time asking Jesus to fill you with himself, his presence, his promise of life. Ask Jesus to reveal himself to you in a fresh way so that you're overflowing with joyful, abundant life.

DAY FIVE: Reflecting on God's Beauty in John's Gospel

After engaging in a Bible study, sometimes it's easy to move on to the next one without taking time to reflect on what God has been communicating to you. Like a traveler on a long road trip, you can wake up and wonder, "Where have I just been?"

1. Spend a few moments flipping through the second half of this study guide (sessions seven through twelve). Which statements or notes did you underline or highlight?

   Why were these meaningful to you?

2. What did you learn through this study that you'd never known before about John's Gospel?

   How do these insights impact your relationship with Jesus?

3. Where have you seen the beauty of God most clearly on display in the Gospel of John?

4. Why is it important to continue pursuing God's beauty in your own life? As you reflect on the stories of Jesus communicated through John's Gospel, where did you see the beauty of God on display?

QUOTABLE

"John's Gospel has rightly been called 'a Gospel of decision.' Every person must choose between light and darkness, faith or unbelief, life or death. Light, life, and salvation, in turn, can be attained only by faith in the crucified and risen Messiah, Jesus."[37]

—Andreas J. Kostenberger

5. The purpose of John's Gospel is to move people toward a robust belief in Jesus Christ. In what ways has your own faith in Jesus been strengthened through this study?

Spend some time thanking God for all that you've learned and discovered through this study about God and his beautiful presence in our world. Ask God for the grace not only to see the beauty of God but also to reflect it in your everyday life.

Endnotes

1. N. T. Wright, *After You Believe: Why Christian Character Matters* (San Francisco: HarperOne, 2010), 62.

2. H. Stephen Shoemaker, *Godstories: New Narratives from Sacred Text* (Valley Forge, Pa.: Judson Press, 1998), xv.

3. www.smithsonianmag.com/science-nature/Galileos-Vision.html.

4. John H. Walton, *The NIV Application Commentary: Genesis* (Grand Rapids: Zondervan, 2001), 231.

5. C. S. Lewis, *God in the Dock: Essays on Theology and Ethics* (Grand Rapids: Eerdmans, 1979), 152–153.

6. Nahum M. Sarna, *Understanding Genesis: The Heritage of Biblical Israel* (New York: Schocken Books, 1966), 30.

7. www.thinkexist.com/quotes/curtis_mcdougall/.

8. Anne Graham Lotz, *The Magnificent Obsession: Embracing the God-Filled Life* (Grand Rapids: Zondervan, 2009), 21.

9. Celia Brewer Sinclair, *Interpretation Bible Studies: Genesis* (Louisville: Westminster John Knox Press, 1999), 40.

10. Walter Brueggemann, *Genesis: A Bible Commentary for Teaching and Preaching* (Atlanta: John Knox Press, 1982), 140.

11. Claus Westermann, *Genesis 12–36: A Commentary* (Minneapolis: Augsburg, 1985), 311.

12. John Calvin, *A Commentary on Genesis*, ed. and trans. J. King (London: Banner of Truth, 1975), 373.

13. www.pbs.org/wgbh/questionofgod/ownwords/mere2.html.

14. Shoemaker, 75.

15. Karen Armstrong, *In the Beginning: A New Interpretation of Genesis* (New York: Ballantine, 1996), 86.

16. John C. L. Gibson, *Genesis*, Daily Study Bible vol. 2 (Philadelphia: Westminster Press, 1982), 200–202.

17. Shoemaker, 75.

18. Nahum M. Sarna, *JPS Torah Commentary: Genesis* (Philadelphia: Jewish Publication Society, 1989), 280.

19. www.sermonsfromseattle.com/series_a_the_beauty_of_god.htm.

20. Michael Card, *The Parable of Joy* (Nashville: Thomas Nelson, 1996), xxi.

21. Many thanks to my dear pastor friend Bill McCready, who responded with this insight in an email on 12/30/10.

22. Leon Morris, *The Gospel According to John: The New International Commentary on the New Testament* (Grand Rapids: Wm. B. Eerdmans, 1971), 254.

23. Jonathan Edwards, *A Treatise Concerning Religious Affections* (reprinted on lulu.com, 2007), 102.

24. http://dictionary.reference.com/browse/blind+spots.

25. Morris, 94.

26. St. Irenaeus, *Against Heresies*, IV, 6:6.

27. Anthony Coniaris, *Do Something Beautiful for God* (Minneapolis: Light and Life Press, 2006), 85.

28. Paul Louis Metzger, *The Gospel of John: When Love Comes to Town* (Downers Grove, Ill.: InterVarsity Press, 2010), 144.

29. http://dictionary.reference.com/browse/abide.

30. Richard Harries, *Art and the Beauty of God: A Christian Understanding* (New York: Mowbray, 1993), 6.

31. William Barclay, *The Gospel of John*, New Daily Study Bible, vol. 2 (Louisville: Westminster John Knox Press, 2001), 231.

32. Morris, 766.

33. N. T. Wright, *Simply Christian: Why Christianity Makes Sense* (San Francisco: HarperOne, 2006), 47.

34. Max Lucado, *The Gospel of John* (Nashville: Thomas Nelson, 2006), 106.

35. Craig R. Koester, *Symbolism in the Fourth Gospel: Meaning, Mystery, Community* (Minneapolis: Fortress Press, 2003), 288.

36. Koester, 121.

37. Andreas J. Kostenberger, *Zondervan Illustrated Bible Backgrounds Commentary: John* (Grand Rapids: Zondervan, 2002), 4.

Bibliography

Genesis

Alexander, T. Desmond and David W. Baker. *Dictionary of the Old Testament Pentateuch.* Downers Grove, Ill.: InterVarsity Press, 2003.

Arthur, Kay. *Teach Me Your Ways: Genesis/Exodus/Leviticus/Numbers/Deuteronomy.* Eugene, Ore.: Harvest House, 1994.

Briscoe, D. Stuart. *The Communicator's Commentary: Genesis.* Waco, Texas: Word, 1987.

Brueggemann, Walter. *Interpretation: Genesis.* Atlanta: John Knox Press, 1982.

Buttrick, George Arthur. *The Interpreter's Bible: General and Old Testament Articles, Genesis and Exodus,* Vol. 1. Nashville: Abingdon, 1980.

Friedman, Richard Elliott. *Commentary on the Torah.* San Francisco: HarperSanFrancisco, 2001.

Hamilton, Victor. *The New International Commentary on the Old Testament: The Book of Genesis, Chapters 1–17.* Grand Rapids: Eerdmans, 1990.

Hummel, Charles and Anne. *Genesis: God's Creative Call.* Downers Grove, Ill.: InterVarsity Press, 2000.

Keck, Leander E., ed. *The New Interpreter's Bible: General and Old Testament Articles, Genesis, Exodus, and Leviticus.* Nashville: Abingdon, 1994.

The Learning Bible (Contemporary English Version). New York: American Bible Society, 2000.

Lucado, Max. *Life Lessons with Max Lucado: Book of Genesis.* Waco, Texas: Word, 1997.

Moyers, Bill. *Genesis: A Living Conversation.* New York: Doubleday, 1996.

Newbigin, Lesslie. *A Walk through the Bible.* Vancouver: Regent College, 1999.

Sarna, Nahum M., ed. *The JPS Torah Commentary: Genesis.* Philadelphia: Jewish Publication Society, 1989.

Shoemaker, H. Stephen. *GodStories: New Narratives from Sacred Texts.* Valley Forge, Pa.: Judson Press, 1998.

Waltke, Bruce K. *Genesis: A Commentary.* Grand Rapids: Zondervan, 2001.

Westermann, Claus. *Genesis 1–11: A Commentary.* Minneapolis: Augsburg, 1974.

Wiesel, Elie. *Messengers of God: Biblical Portraits and Legends*, trans. Marion Wiesel. New York: Random House, 1976.

Williams, Michael E., ed. *The Storyteller's Companion to the Bible: Genesis*, Vol. 1. Nashville: Abingdon, 1991.

John

Bailey, Kenneth E. *Jesus through Middle Eastern Eyes: Cultural Studies in the Gospels*. Downers Grove, Ill.: InterVarsity Press, 2008.

Blackaby, Henry, Richard Blackaby, Thomas Blackaby, Melvin Blackaby, and Norman Blackaby. *Encounters with God: John, Small Group Study*. Nashville: Thomas Nelson, 2007.

Blomberg, Craig L. *The Historical Reliability of the Gospels*, second ed. Downers Grove, Ill.: InterVarsity Press, 2007.

Blomberg, Craig L. *Preaching the Parables: From Responsible Interpretation to Powerful Proclamation*. Grand Rapids: Baker, 2004.

Brown, Raymond E. *The Gospel According to John XII-XXI: A New Translation with Introduction and Commentary*. Vol. 29A. New Haven: Yale University Press, 1970.

Burge, Gary M. *The NIV Application Commentary: John*. Grand Rapids: Zondervan, 2000.

Card, Michael. *The Parable of Joy*. Nashville: Thomas Nelson, 1995.

Connelly, Douglas. *John: The Way to True Life*. Downers Grove, Ill.: InterVarsity Press, 2002.

Fredrikson, Roger L. *The Communicator's Commentary: John*. Waco, Texas: Word, 1985.

Koester, Craig R. *Symbolism in the Fourth Gospel: Meaning, Mystery, Community*, second ed. Minneapolis: Fortress Press, 2003.

Kostenberger, Andreas J. *Zondervan Illustrated Bible Backgrounds Commentary: John*. Grand Rapids: Zondervan, 2002.

The Learning Bible (Contemporary English Version). New York: American Bible Society, 2000.

Longman III, Tremper and David E. Garland, eds. *The Expository Bible Commentary: Luke–Acts*, rev. ed. Vol. 10. Grand Rapids: Zondervan, 2007.

Lucado, Max. *The Gospel of John*. Nashville: Thomas Nelson, 2006.

MacArthur, John. *John: Jesus—the Word, the Messiah, the Son of God*. Nashville: Thomas Nelson, 2007.

Matson, Mark A. *Interpretation Bible Studies: John*. Louisville: Westminster John Knox Press, 2002.

Metzger, Paul Louis. *The Gospel of John: When Love Comes to Town*. Downers Grove, Ill.: InterVarsity Press, 2010.

Sloyan, Gerard S. *John: Interpretation, a Bible Commentary for Teaching and Preaching*. Atlanta: John Knox Press, 1988.

Swindoll, Charles R. *Swindoll's New Testament Insights: John*. Grand Rapids: Zondervan, 2010.

About the Author

Host of the popular podcast, *The Joycast*, Margaret Feinberg is a Bible teacher and speaker at churches and leading conferences. Her books, including *More Power To You* and *Taste and See: Discovering God Among Butchers, Bakers and Fresh Food Makers*, and her Bible studies have sold over one million copies and received critical acclaim and extensive national media coverage from the Associated Press, *USA Today*, and more.

She was named one of 50 women most shaping culture and the church today by *Christianity Today*. Margaret lives in Utah with her husband, Leif, and their superpup, Zoom. She believes some of the best days are spent around a table with amazing food and friends.

Join her on Instagram and Facebook @mafeinberg.